To Be a Politician

Stimson Bullitt

To Be
a
Politician

Introduction by David Riesman

1959

Doubleday & Company, Inc., Garden City, New York

to Kay

▼

ACKNOWLEDGMENTS

I declare thanks to John Damski and Walter Walkinshaw for their criticism of parts of the manuscript; and to Alain and Rosemary Enthoven, Jon and Sally Goldmark, and Ancil H. Payne for their critical advice on much of the text, their help largely consisting of requests for clarification of obscure passages, to the meaning of which even their high intelligence could not penetrate. A number of the ideas first were formed or developed in the course of correspondence with Jerry Berlin. These friends' generous attention to the work in process encouraged me to proceed with the job. Katharine M. Bullitt contributed in every way throughout the progress of this work.

▼

FOREWORD

As a former politician, blessed with leisure and obscurity, I reflect upon the calling which has absorbed me. This book examines the life led by politicians, their conditions of labor, habits of mind, the qualities which their work demands, and some of their trade secrets. Comparing their vocation as a way of life with private pursuits, it looks at the changing relationship between citizen and politician and the effects of this on the process of government. It considers the quality of truth in politics. It considers what it is to be a politician.

May the boundary between the roles of citizen and politician be made low but sharp? May it be put low enough to be more easily crossed on the way back to private life, so that politics as a temporary profession may not deter the entry of men good enough to have something to lose? Yet, at the same time, can the line be drawn so as clearly to define a politician's role during the present condition of overlapping functions between his own and other vocations in the management of affairs?

What effect does personality have on the communication between citizen and politician? What bearing do certain aspects of personality have on a politician's value and success? What kind of personality in a politician can enable him best to reconcile his duties of democratic leadership—the duty to give direction and the duty to be responsive? How are the qualities of independent character and inner purpose in a politician related to the problem of serving the public and obtaining its support yet also providing guidance?

Can we obtain definiteness rather than isolation in a politician's personality, diversity among politicians instead of dispersion? How do these qualities affect the politician's performance in office and the flavor which he gives to his constituents? How does his flavor shape his constituents' attitudes toward him? An outlook common among some politicians is that the duty to give effect to the public's current wishes forbids the exercise of his conscience or judgment; this belief tends toward merging the roles of governing and governed; the tendency is reinforced by the supposition that since no man is an island one might as well become part of the sea.

Refusing to assume that man is born to trouble or to nothing more than cultivated comfort, a politician can aspire to a better scheme of things, a scheme which might be brought to pass with politicians' help. But most utopias cannot be reached, and of the rest most are found wanting when attained at last. Pursuit is arduous for a politician because these golden lands recede before him, as the sparks fly upward from a campfire, disappearing in the dark. Thus a politician's service as a part-time pilgrim depends at least on public acceptance of him in this part. A central question of a politician's conduct is how he can fulfill today's needs and wishes of those to whom he owes a duty, while he keeps his singularity and tries to lead his constituents toward his vision of an exalted polity; how he can be a man after their own heart, yet listen for a drum beyond their earshot and "step to the music which he hears, however measured or far away."

My intention is not to encourage those who consider entering politics either to go in or stay out. It is to give them comprehension with which to make their choice. The purpose of this book is not to persuade anyone to respect politicians or even to give them pity or affection and thus more easily to suffer them. My aim is to give the reader better understanding of this profession so that when he measures a politician's character and record of performance he may apply standards which not only fit what is and what can be done, but also are a guide for what a politician ought to do and be.

▼

CONTENTS

3

QUALITIES

4

LEADERSHIP AMONG THE LEISURED

▼

INTRODUCTION

This is a book by a practicing lawyer, a Democrat of some political experience (mostly in his home state of Washington), little given to cant. Aspiring politicians who, like the author, are young, literate, and either amateur or idealistic or both, can learn much from it; professional students of political behavior, in and out of the universities, can also learn from it; and so can the great audience of citizens who might get better service from politicians if they understood the limits and opportunities of the profession, and for whom in any event the understanding of political life can make what happens in the world more meaningful if not less tragic.

It has not been uncommon for leading American politicians to write their memoirs, often bulky tomes like James G. Blaine's *Twenty Years of Congress,* in which defeat for high office might be somewhat assuaged by polemics and apologias. Former Presidents have fought off creditors and history by the same route. Cabinet ministers have been prolific—though perhaps few have confided to their diaries as much of their daily grist as Harold Ickes, one of those many politicians whose vanity (a theme Mr. Bullitt treats at length) seems to have been a principal source of their strength and rectitude. I know, however, few memoirs by men who did not hold high office (Ed Flynn's *You're the Boss* is both more and less than a memoir), and still fewer by young men who still have political hopes: though in intellectual life it is now customary to write one's autobiography or political testament while still in early middle life (witness, for example, Stephen Spender, Dwight MacDonald, Mary McCarthy), a candidate for office hesitates to put ammunition in the enemy's hands, and is in addition usually much too busy. How busy, in fact, Mr. Bullitt makes amply plain in these pages.

To be sure, Mr. Bullitt is not writing autobiography here, quite; rather, he is writing essays which draw on his experience of what it is like to be a politician—about the company the politician keeps, the ethical dilemmas he faces, the encounters that wound, that educate, and that inspire. Though I have not met him, I feel from this book that I have a sense of his qualities: a salty man, without false heartiness; a brave man, without false heroics; a thoughtful man, without pretensions. What distinguishes him is the capacity to confront the experiences of turmoil the politician has, especially during campaigns, while saving something of himself for reflection and perspective: to be at once insider and outsider.

It occurred to me, realizing that Mr. Bullitt's father had also been a politician, that having the opportunity to observe at home may have helped give him a certain skeptical, matter-of-fact, unawed attitude toward public affairs. Skepticism, of course, is not at all the same as cynicism, the latter being simply a formula for escaping the risks of judgment. In fact, one of the themes of this book concerns the cultivation of a certain degree of detachment while eschewing cynicism: by finding friends who are not "important" and don't consider political success important; by having another career, such as the law, to fall back upon; and by a love for reading, partly as a sheer diversion and partly as one source for helping to understand and assimilate experience.

Mr. Bullitt shares with his readers the experiences of campaigning where, despite all the tools of public opinion and motivation research, the candidate is almost helpless to gauge the effect of particular moves, speeches, poses, advertisements, and hence tends to be a sucker for all sorts of energetic and expensive nostrums urged by his friends or by the example of his enemies.

While the voting studies done in national campaigns by Professor Paul F. Lazarsfeld and his associates have suggested that presidential campaigns seldom change many votes and only marginally increase turnout, local campaigns, where interest is slight, are another story; in any case, the situation remains one in which each candidate has to campaign because the others do, because he must support his supporters, and because he can never be sure and hence inclines to flee forward into activity. (Of course, Mr. Bullitt's first primary campaign for Congress was different, because he was unknown and had to become, so to speak, a brand name before being allowed to carry his party's name.) During the campaign, not only does the candidate tend to lose his head, but he becomes utterly surfeited with people, including his close friends on whom he nevertheless depends. Mr. Bullitt points out that this is not the case with those who, like Franklin Roosevelt, feed on people without strain and glut; and there are other politicians who are people-addicted. But surfeit is unavoidable for those who, being capable of attachment to people, do not meet them with wholly studied or wholly unstudied impersonality; for such men, of whom Mr. Bullitt is almost certainly an example, each human contact takes its human toll in the course of the endless handshakings at factory gates and in homes—encounters for which a sensitive person must brace himself like a reluctant salesman.

Indeed, hardly any of the politician's ethical or tactical problems are unique to him, save in degree; a teacher, for instance, aware of his complex relations with students, his dependence on them, his fear to move them from their moorings, can react empathically to Mr. Bullitt's account of how the politician must be at once teacher and propagandist, speaking to people's given needs while uncovering potential ones. And what he says about the emptiness of successful politicians, who have grown so accustomed to speaking for effect and to associating with men of power that they are no longer themselves distinct individuals— this is surely the experience many have with important men in

business and the professions, even though in the latter self-
selection and conditioning require less surrender of privacy and
hence of self. So, too, Mr. Bullitt observes how seldom politicians
can afford sexual or other time-consuming vices, simply because
the pursuit of success keeps them too busy for much self-indulgence; although he also notes that that pursuit, by alienating a
man from his family and traditional ties and by heightening the
pressures upon him, is likely to induct him into the easy adulteries
that tempt celebrities. (To pursue gross appetites in the legendary
way Boies Penrose did requires either rule by divine right of party
and big or little business or a constituency which admires
"*machismo*," such as Huey Long or Senator McCarthy had.)

One of the contributions of this book is, in fact, to show how
politicians and their constituents are becoming more similar with
time, with the former differing in being more ambitious, more
energetic, and even more gregarious. As the general level of education rises, politics serves decreasingly as a second chance at big
stakes for an uneducated man; for analogous reasons it less often
opens a career for men, whether well educated or not, who rise
by representing a downtrodden group. For instance, in an earlier
day Irishmen in New England found politics an available route
to the big money—but the sons and grandsons of such men can
study engineering at Notre Dame or political theory at Harvard,
leaving minor political rank to the Italians, who may in turn leave
it to the Bullitts, thus completing a cycle. As the middle class
absorbs more and more Americans, politicians will tend to come
from this class and to represent it—even, in their moderation,
amiability, and fear of offending, to overrepresent it.

In spite of this tendency toward homogenization, the overgen-
eralized and traditional disdain and deprecation of politicians
hang on. Having read Lincoln Steffens early, I grew up without
this disdain, but found when I began teaching law twenty years
ago that my students, and markedly so the better they were, held
politicians in complete contempt. I looked around then for books
which would reveal both the essential humanity and decency of

many politicians and the inescapable functions they performed, and did not find many (J. T. Salter's *Boss Rule* was one), and Mr. Bullitt's would have been an enormous help. The view the students held, and so many still hold, deprives public life both of needed actors and a critical audience—for how can an audience be critical if it assumes to start with the view that all stagecraft is mere illusion put on by charlatans? This view is dangerous, too, because it opens the path for men to succeed in politics by claiming not only to be above racketeering and favor-jobbing but also to be above party, above politics—as totalitarian leaders have characteristically done: people, both leaders and led, who are active in politics without admitting the fact usually evade the ethical issues of action and responsibility either by knavery or naïveté. And then I have always disliked the snobbery with which Americans have viewed politicians (though I don't feel that the reverse sentimentality of *The Last Hurrah* is much improvement). The moral indignation expended on "politics" and politicians is seldom innocent. And it is generally unjust, for I share Mr. Bullitt's opinion that on the whole (though hardly in my home state of Illinois, at present) our representatives, especially if they draw on a district of some heterogeneity of interests, give more disinterested and less parochial service than we ask or expect of them; and there are many congressmen of broad horizons who represent voters who neither know of their best work nor would care about it if they did.

It is to the essential task of separating the problems of politics as a generic calling (in Max Weber's sense) from those of politicians in the American grain that Mr. Bullitt addresses himself with wit, learning, and casuistical sensibility. One of his most important discussions presents his judgment that it is impractical to propose a radical or complex idea during a campaign, for in the heat of the fight any such idea will be sure to be rejected (as Stevenson's sensible proposal on H-bombs was rejected). I was especially struck by this, since I had urged on some of the members of Stevenson's entourage my conviction that he couldn't possibly be elected, and that he therefore had a magnificent opportunity to educate his fellow-Americans, as well as to help prepare a cadre of discerning devotees for the next campaign and the next. On this and other occasions, I have been defeated by the belief surrounding a candidate that he must act as if he were sure to win—partly perhaps reflecting the tradition of American sports and partly a more general difficulty of Americans in keeping the long-run and the short-run both in mind at once. Mr. Bullitt himself regards a campaign as inevitably oriented to the short-run and, through plain, unsubtle talk, as mobilizing inevitably heterogeneous support. At the same time, he is aware of the insidious charms for a campaigner of the rationale that to educate later, he must win now; though this be true, he insists that it never justifies deception or McCarthyite tactics or a disingenuous presentation of one's past; and I wish he had discussed more at length why on some occasions these rules are adhered to, while on others (for instance, even among fair-minded Englishmen, the Zinoviev letter, or the devaluation of the pound) they break down. But a campaigner in Mr. Bullitt's view need not be incontinent: he need not say all he hopes to accomplish in office, though he may safely say more and should say more than most politicians do about his very general hopes for the region or the country at large. In brief compass, Mr. Bullitt differentiates between honesty, which a politician should possess, and sincerity, which can be deceptive: the former quality springs from commitment; the latter, from excessive permeability to others.

Plainly enough, a politician who conducts himself as Mr. Bullitt believes is in keeping with his calling will sometimes lose elections, though he is not likely also to mislead the voters (nor is he bound to assume a rigid posture of virtue to ensure defeat and then to solace it with self-righteousness). What then? The defeated politician is like the defeated union leader in having no assured berth to return to—one reason, of course, why both sometimes resort to gangster tactics or demagogy to stay in office (whereas businessmen who lose out, for instance in proxy fights, are usually well paid for their pains). Even if the defeated politician has private means, he needs work to restore his self-confidence and sense of being competent at something. If he is a teacher, he has a hard time returning to the academy—just as does a university president ousted by trustees; Mr. Bullitt notes that it is feared the ex-politician as teacher may corrupt the young. If he is a businessman, he is not likely to be welcome back at the office—unlike the dollar-a-year man who brings back valuable know-how and contacts. Law practice, Mr. Bullitt suggests, is less useful as a springboard to politics than as a shelter from it (as a judgeship can be a shelter from both): it is one of the few professions where, unlike for example medicine or architecture, absence does not mean getting rusty, for in a small office the work is not that specialized and the qualities needed for success include far more than technical *expertise*. Law, like any intensive alternative career, gives the defeated candidate a chance to reveal other aspects of himself than campaigning did, and thus to remind himself and others that he is still the same, and his own, man.

Of course, maintenance of such an escape hatch depends on the ability of at least some clients to separate the candidate's views from the professional man's opinions, and thus on a climate of legal practice in which lawyers are relatively free to take causes and cases without being overidentified with them. There is evidence that it has become somewhat more difficult for lawyers to retain this sort of independence; at times, those who have defended people accused of Communism or disloyalty have suffered guilt by association, even when appointed by the Court or the Bar Association. And in general, the kind of law practice which permits freedom, by not depending on a single big client or type of client, requires much judgment and some sacrifice to develop: in professional, as in intellectual, life it is all too easy to get typed, and all too comfortable. Mr. Bullitt does not speak of this directly, but has apparently managed to practice both law and politics, for every even-numbered year since 1946 (when he got out of

service) he has been out campaigning for himself or for other
candidates.

Furthermore, he sees the advantage in what he terms enforced
sabbaticals for politicians. In part, just because politicians are
educator-entertainers, the audience will demand new performance with new personalities even to teach the same things. (Their
insistence may be all the greater because the show, like that on
TV, appears to be free.) The politician himself needs contact with
a great variety of spheres of life if he is to have empathy with
the problems of the voiceless as well as the noisy among his constituents (the private and sheltered person, too, can find in politics a way of acculturation to the gamut of cultures and classes
which our society still encapsulates despite in some respects
growing uniformity). Even so, Mr. Bullitt recognizes that specialization and experience count, in politics as elsewhere, and that
rotation in office deprives practitioners of these advantages.

At the same time, politics as a profession forces people con-
stantly into the company of bores, and with fewer mechanisms
for keeping them at a distance (such as the doctor's stethoscope,
the sociologist's interview) than some other professions provide.
Thus, Mr. Bullitt writes:

"For a man of active intellect the most severe condition of politics is
to abstain from the full and constant use of his powers. He must be
willing to submit to boredom and make the effort to conceal it. Insofar
as a politician works in his party organization his patience is taxed
by tedium such as service on committees engaged in administration
(e.g. organizing a dinner meeting or picnic), a function suited to a
single person. Most political meetings are dull enough to spur the
ambition of impatient men. By custom, a private has to sit through
them in silence, an officer is allowed to speak, and a general may
arrive at the end to make the main oration during which he may while
away the time by listening to his own voice."

And what about the wives of politicians who can be immensely
helpful in campaigns but must often attend meetings without the
break in monotony that comes from speaking at them? Politics

seems to me one of those callings where celibacy can be defended on practical grounds. For while the wives of some kinds of doctors and executives must put up with irregular hours and tense lives, and while the wives of college presidents must sit through many boring rituals, all these women have at least the modest compensations bought by their spouses' high income and success. Politicians, however, along with ministers and school officials, can but seldom give their wives an anxiety-free middle-class existence—and all these occupations select men who are not immune to the feelings even of the women and children around them (while surgeons and manufacturers are sometimes quite immune). This hardship on and exploitation of the wives and children of people in some service occupations seems to me one good reason for raising salaries in these fields (the notion that more money will recruit more qualified people is open to question).

If the politician's ties with family are often problematic and tenuous so, as already indicated, are ties with friends. This is partly ecological: the politician moves around a lot—to the state capital (often in a provincial town) and to Washington (a still provincial town); there is high turnover among those in the same trajectory; and, again like the school superintendent, or union leader, or college president, his eminence is of a particularly isolated sort: he can befriend his subordinates more readily than he can be friends with them, and he has few true colleagues who are not also rivals in a small world. Moreover, a politician's friend is tempted to play the role of coach—even to exaggerating the malice of the· enemy, as Mr. Bullitt says, "to make him a more fiercely aggressive campaigner." And the very climate we have been discussing, in which decent and sometimes even quite thoughtful people automatically despise politicians (their best friends are invariably "statesmen"), makes the friends of a politician either the most threatening of pressure groups, ready to withdraw love rather than votes, or the readiest to be disillusioned about a man whom they could accept only by not appraising him and his situation realistically. Indeed, if the friends of politicians will only read this book, they will have a chance to become not only more critical but also more charitable.

So far, I have stressed some of the poignancies of political life that are reflected in Mr. Bullitt's book—in part, no doubt, because of my own bias in favor of politicians. But Mr. Bullitt's own tone is not primarily sad; rather, it is skeptical, wry, alive. He recognizes that politicians, if less philosophical than some professors, are more so than most businessmen and that, though they are seldom off duty, they are accustomed to speak their minds at least as freely as the latter. In fact, their trade exposes them to the expectation that they *should* have opinions on most issues—they cannot always be ducking and evading—and, like lawyers, they exist in a dialectical atmosphere (not for them the frequent social taboo against "talking politics or religion"!). It is not so much their views as their personalities which have to be smooth; concerning the latter, Mr. Bullitt observes that few politicians of his acquaintance, whatever their public image, are sharply etched and idiosyncratic as people: their style becomes increasingly undifferentiated.

These changes are in part the result of the relaxation of social-class tensions to which I have referred earlier: the general increase of wealth and the concomitant loss of rigid distinctions make it difficult to maintain the Madisonian bases for political diversity, or to recruit politicians who speak for the residual oppressed strata; with the virtual shutting off of immigration from Europe and the continuing horizontal mobility within this country, these tendencies will grow in strength. Politicians must still put together—and sunder—interest groups, ethnic blocs, and other amalgams, but their own heterogeneity declines along with that of their constituents. Moreover, with the increasing demands on the politician, based on crescent population and interdependence, and on the intensities generated by the mass media, the career becomes too strenuous to attract the well-born drone—a type on the wane even in the South, as occupational choice more and more becomes based on talent and formal education rather than on birth or tradition. Perhaps, in fact, politics is especially strenuous for the well-born person, who must learn humility toward constituents and the organization and must acquire a certain kind of toughness in which insults and vulgarity neither inhibit nor fascinate him. (I rather suspect that Mr. Bullitt cultivated some of these qualities by learning to box in school and college; I have known of a number of sensitive men who, by learning to box or play football, gained an unshakable confidence in encounters unmediated by rank—and of a few who, like Theodore Roosevelt, turned self-defense into a way of life.) The politician who is not single-minded, who has not specialized his emotions around the concerns of an oppressed but carefully hidden ego, will seldom succeed in competition with the Sammy who never stops running; indeed, despite all talk of free enterprise, business is not nearly so competitive.

Business as a whole, however, as Mr. Bullitt points out, competes with politics as a whole, all too successfully, in providing entertaining alternatives for leisure time. The politician, like the minister, has seen his role as popular entertainer-*cum*-educator give way to the mass media and those consumer goods, including suburbanism as a way of life, which the media make attractive. At the same time, politics in the age of nuclear fission has become even more urgent than hitherto, and its very seriousness is a drawback in competing with commercial or do-it-yourself entertainment, particularly among an electorate that expects to be amused but also, having become more literate and sophisticated, is not so readily amused as in the days of long sermons and courthouse antics. In this situation, politicians feel compelled to ally themselves with the media, at enormous expense in money and in self-manipulation, if they are to be noticed and to have a chance to interpret and affect the events the media announce. Certainly, they can no longer fall back on traditional hegemonies of station, information, and verbal facility, for all these are now widely shared and democratized. What they do fall back on is their personal flavor or *charisma*—a bedside manner which is often the only diagnostic skill they have. Mr. Bullitt writes:

"While directness of purpose and capacity for superior work are, as always, the main assets required for reaching the top, the lack of inherited gifts of rank and circumstance is being replaced as a barrier to political success by the lack of moderation, sincerity, and warmth. The latter makes political 4F's of some men and women who as politicians would do public good. The decline in the importance of party organization has made it easier for a man to succeed in politics without the skills of working with an organization, yet it has made it harder for him to overcome the absence of the vendible elements of personality. He has to get along with everyone because it is no longer enough to get along with fellow party members alone. One result is to admit to office politicians who have energy, ability, and charm, yet lack purpose about anything beyond their own careers. Leo Durocher said about big league baseball, 'Nice guys finish last,' but in politics they often finish first."

They finish first, in part, because the nice citizen who is lured into voting either by a particular candidate's personality or because he regards voting as a kind of minimal civic decency is not likely to care about issues. Morris Janowitz's analysis of consent and manipulation in national elections, based on survey data, reveals that those voters who feel least involved rely most heavily on "personality" as the basis of choice. My friend, Lewis Dexter, who has been a precinct worker and poller in many campaigns, tells me that a congressman's votes on even the most hotly debated legislation are seldom known in his home territory, let alone count as a factor in his re-election (save as such votes open the purses of wealthy backers or, more occasionally, as a particular stand wins the enthusiasm of hard-working people who can marshal a group of voters). Mr. Bullitt's own experience as a campaigner is identical: in accosting prospective voters at factory gates, taverns, street corners, and shopping centers, he found that he hardly ever was questioned about a stand he had taken. Many whom he approached were indifferent; some feared that the approach was from a bum or a drunk—and some that it was from

someone who wanted to warn them that they live in a dangerous
world where some choices are more difficult than deciding which
horse to bet on (one can only lose votes by campaigning at a
track) or which jar of peaches to buy (at a shopping center people are relatively receptive to a candidate, being in leisurely and
unfrightened spirits). Mr. Bullitt discovered what all interviewers
know, namely, that one really hostile encounter takes away the
joy and confidence built on forty amiable ones—perhaps because,
like a nightmare, it is a reminder of hidden reefs in nature, society, or in one's own personality. Yet one goes back into the fray
because, of course, one believes that one's victory matters, but
beyond that because one is campaigning and if one stopped to
ask at each moment *"cui bono?"* the race itself and all the acts
and incantations on behalf of victory might not seem too important. And anyway, as in a battle, one is being shot at by
enemies while surrounded by comrades: one would have to be
sick to beg off.

Nevertheless, Mr. Bullitt does ask *"cui bono?"* and he skirts
as close to an answer as many social scientists and novelists have
done. He notices that ambition, if not overpowering, can be a
kind of substitute for character: it can force people to do un-
pleasant things and, if the rules of the game are clear and well
enforced, keep the contest within bounds. And he realizes how
hard it is for Western man, put on a racecourse, not to run—even
while capable of simultaneous awareness that it is absurd.

Mr. Bullitt has written a book on what it takes, and takes out
of one, to be a liberal politician in the urban Northwest. He makes
clear what many dimly realize, namely, that the basis of political representation has today become too parochial, tying every
elected man except the President to a gerrymandered district at
the expense of larger entities. He notes that congressmen are all
too likely to be small-town small-timers, due to a fossil localism
that requires men to live (or at least pretend to) in the districts
from which they stand for election; and many districts possess
no decent college or other civilized center (it would help if one

could group congressmen regionally, as one can do with candidates for Rhodes Scholarships). And I would myself add that America, as the world shrinks, becomes only a larger parish, cosmopolitan enough to pretend it isn't one; national borders are gerrymandered, too, and their transcendence requires the enlargement and reinterpretation of our ideas of representation. Had Mr. Bullitt not been washed out of the race for Congress in 1952, he might well have become a leader in the House and shown himself to be a practical and reflective idealist, energetic enough to serve both his constituents and his country and, beyond these, that voteless and all too voiceless constituency: the planet and the unborn.

David Riesman

Part

1

The Profession

▼

1

POLITICS AS A CALLING

To enjoy politics one must enjoy people; it helps if one likes them as well. A politician wants and tries to like people. He must be with them, and a friendly relationship makes it easier for him to satisfy and please. He meets and works with every kind. He is enabled to associate with the best, and compelled by duty and circumstance to spend time with some of the worst. Near the centers of government, which has come to reach us all, he is invited to open almost any door; and the universal franchise makes him practice unrestricted social intercourse. His uncommon relationship to people requires him to develop a singular attitude toward them. He must be sensitive to all aspects of their personalities, including their changing opinions of him, yet be numb to the pain of their rebukes.

A politician should feel at home in both the abstract and the concrete. He needs to think along the boundary between the general propositions of the schoolroom or the cloister and the specific problems of the business office or the shop. To get along in politics a man's inclinations should be balanced between people and ideas. A man too concerned with people may lack judgment in his decisions of public policy, and campaign for office as though he were in a popularity contest. One who puts too much emphasis on issues tends to forget his fellow citizens, each of them, whose welfare is the object of his work. Free from the facts of human needs, here and now, he risks becoming dogmatic. His grand designs may so enchant him that he forces others to accommodate themselves to the symmetrical perfection of his program. Countries like China, France, and Russia in their periods of revolution tend to be afflicted by those hard men who try to impose a platform as an iron frame, while America suffers from the men who would rather be loved.

It is impossible to master or even learn a great deal about all the subjects to be tackled—war, peace, education, money, labor, preservation of national monuments, disposition of useless papers . . . It would take a universal genius to be expert in all. An able politician is neither an amateur nor a specialist. He is a general practitioner.

There is less difference now between a politician's work and the work of those who manage society in other fields. In antiquity, the skills and functions of the military, business, and government were united in one man, as in some Roman leaders who in one career would manage farms, administer a province, negotiate a treaty, judge disputes, collect rents, debate laws, and march on Antioch at a legion's head. Then for a long time these skills and functions were apart. The Confederacy's performance was impaired by combining in Jefferson Davis both military and political strategy. Conversely, their separation benefited the Union, whose generals either admitted or demonstrated their unfitness for politics. Now these functions are merging again. The change tends to be more drastic for the officer and executive than for the politician, who has long been attending to a little of everything. This extension of his range has made a politician's knowledge even broader and more shallow. Having children and trying to answer their questions is a good preparation for a politician, who must deal with many things he does not understand.

In the political world the grasp of abstract ideas is better than it is in business, but not so good as in the university. Among politicians the comprehension of specific problems is also intermediate, not so good as it is among businessmen but better than it is among academics. Writing of politicians, Macaulay declared: "The perfect lawgiver is a just temper between the mere man of theory, who can see nothing but general principles, and the mere man of business, who can see nothing but particular circumstances." Although the average politician's mentality is below that in some other professions, in politics one can acquire a better comprehension of the forest, together with its trees, than in any other field.

An American politician does a job and plays a part. He serves as both a craftsman and a symbol. The higher public offices bear more moral and emotional color in the public eye than other occupations, except perhaps that of the clergy.

A superior politician combines two contrasting qualities: In the details of his work he is flexible, yet the outlines of his personality are definite. The flexibility is necessary to do justice under the democratic process, and also to permit him to survive in politics. His nature must be clearly enough defined for him to know who he is, so that his policies may be guided by some rational framework of principles as well as for his satisfaction with himself. Few great public men have differed from this pattern, and in none of them was it reversed—none was without direction or identity yet stiff in execution of detail. But the proportion of those in politics who have a well-defined character is exaggerated in the public mind, because a visible sign is often mistaken for proof of an inward grace. Evidence only, and often overrated, is a forelock, a brown derby, red suspenders, or an underslung pipe.

▼

A constituent's patriotic idealism or self-esteem is shown by his disappointment at a politician's failure to meet the standards of merit which the constituent thinks deserved by his country, his community, or himself. But from this falling short of an ideal standard, for the citizen to presume his representative's inferiority to politicians of another time or place (whose merits he has heard of or imagined) is to confuse an expectation with a wish. If his clay-footed Senator is one of the Senate's best, he should recognize the depressing fact. To appreciate comparative worth

ans is to face reality and to give them their due,
ide when the foreigner asked, "Who is France's
and he replied, "Victor Hugo, alas."

because politicians are regarded as necessary evils, both their conduct and existence are condoned. It is thought that by the necessities of his profession a soldier must kill and a politician lie. Most American citizens are given better government than they realize, and most politicians are better public servants than many people think. The more complete and accurate information which citizens now receive about candidates and their records tends to eliminate the worst knaves and fools from among elected officials. In general, as in other fields, the quality has improved as the profession has grown more competitive, although the magnitude of the problems has increased faster than the average quality of the membership has risen.

One cause of the disparity between popular belief and fact is ignorance of how much a politician is affected by his instinct of workmanship and his desire to be liked, respected, and re-elected. People are confused by their contradictory attitudes toward public leadership: On the one hand there is the notion that most politicians are rascals, based partly on substantial evidence of it in the period following the Civil War; on the other hand is the admiration for institutions of government, compounded of reverence for tradition and pride in the merits of the city, state, or nation as symbolized in its government. It is not generally realized that politicians are steeped in the same patriotic myth that is common to all other citizens who grew up in this country. The mansions and temples of government in state capitals and in Washington encourage upright conduct as well as vanity.

The most dramatic demonstration of the influence on politicians of this patriotic myth is the Presidency. On entering it, a man will raise the level of his performance sharply, unless he does not clearly understand what is expected of him. Not only is he inspired to surpass himself but also he is free from concern about self-preservation and, on the whole, from temptation to promote immediate selfish aims. This is by reason of the sign which could be displayed above the White House door: "Banish hope of further advancement (except in the history books) ye who enter here."

▼

To enter politics at the bottom is easy and good sense. Competition is mild, and one may practice in an arena where unseasoned judgment is not fatal. Among professionals, however, the game is played for keeps. Survival depends on quick resourcefulness and judgment which come partly from experience. A few people in public life but not in politics can, like Mrs. Roosevelt, make up for lack of cunning by common sense and purity of heart. The danger line is crossed when a man starts to appear in the papers. From then on he will be saddled with his record and penalized for his unpopular companions or unfortunate remarks. On the Congressional level the players are skilled, most of them seasoned by years in minor leagues. The only way to learn the system well is to see its whole range. Those who enter politics late in life, and start in high office, are led by ignorance into errors which are avoided by those who realize the nature and significance of the work done by people down the line.

The most important reason for starting as a part-time apprentice is that one may at the same time learn politics and another trade. The risk is slight that one will stay an amateur so long that he becomes a dabbler. The choice does not matter much, but a private calling is essential to the politician who is brave and wishes to be free. Like Cincinnatus, he should have a plow standing ready for him in a field at home. This goes for everyone, despite the independence of his means. A strong-willed politician's flesh is too weak not to be chilled by the prospect of a long drop. Without a happy alternative, an acrobat's net, he cannot afford the independent judgment which he must have to do his duty. Through the window he sees the old men sitting on the courthouse lawn; unless he can afford to lose he may think, "There . . . go I," and keep a wetted finger in the air. Such service to constituents is less than they deserve, although they may be given what some of them demand. And on those terms politics is not worth its price. The Book of Common Prayer addresses God, "whose service is perfect freedom." But base obedience to others' whims dissolves a man's identity by his immersion in the mass.

▼

To succeed in American politics, one must win the acceptance of many people and the approval of some, but compared to other fields the approval needs to be more widespread and need not be as strong. As always, success depends both on circumstances of background and situation, and on personal qualities. But the balance has shifted to favor personal qualities. Accidents of prejudice or birth are smaller factors now, except for a Negro or a Roosevelt. A distinguished origin, such as a Mayflower ancestor or a log cabin, is worth less now than it was before, while qualities of ability and personality and experience common to the voters are worth more. Scandal among one's kin is not much of a handicap except for a candidate for local office in a small town.

Some people have substantial advantages available to them in the form of status, connections, or inherited wealth, factors not a part of their own personality or the result of their own efforts. In many situations, if one's gifts of privilege are used to further personal aims, one's talents atrophy because they are not whetted on other people's skills. On the other hand, if a person's outward gifts are used either not at all or only toward ends unconnected with his career, he misses the chance to put himself closer to a spot where his inner gifts will be most effective. In fact, the time spent in diversions to collateral ends is a handicap in competition with those who focus on a single goal. A person who uses money for play, status for security, and connections for social pleasure, tends to lose out to one who has none of these but puts all his time on his career's advance.

And where is the line to be drawn? For the son of a general or the child of a successful doctor or lawyer who follows the same profession it seems the correct course to avail himself of all such outside advantages. A man who stays within the shelter of his family business is not likely to develop unless he runs the firm, rather than working for it, and unless it must compete, instead of being just a collection of investments. In politics it is wise to make full use of those advantages which are outside one's self and which mankind has chosen to applaud so much less than those gifts which happen, equally by chance, to be located within us. Politics is so competitive that there is no risk that a person's powers will decay if he employs his outward gifts to help him toward success.

▼

Among politicians one finds cowardice, dishonesty, and pride, but little sloth, lust, cruelty, or greed. Contrary to popular fiction, Americans eminent in the management of affairs make poor symbols of evil. We refuse to elevate Caligulas and Borgias, who "drink iniquity like water." Although some politicians have colorful personalities, few successful ones have lurid faults.

In politics, voluptuaries are even more uncommon than ascetics. Ambition makes most successful politicians impose on themselves disciplined habits of restraint from vicious pleasures. They have little time for self-indulgence. Even when they have a moment with nothing to do but degrade themselves, they generally can resist temptation because they prefer success to pleasure. To obtain the secrecy necessary for vice is often more inconvenient for them than for obscure men. However, some high-ranking politicians are promiscuous with women. After long neglect, their wives tend to cool toward them. They are away from home much of the time and often drink enough to forget some of their duties when an opportunity comes to hand. Because they are celebrated figures the flattery shown by their favor is a substitute for time-consuming preliminary pursuit. Some female campaign workers combine frustration with hero worship. But the main cause, these men's driving egos, overshadows the supplemental causes. They take women not for pleasure but as one of the signs

'usive club memberships and addressing big
'mes. Their practice proves the narrowness
adth of their interests. Denied the ancient
ushing underlings around and the chance to take
on peers, these men would feel they were missing out if
ey did not indulge in the surviving prerogatives of rank which
remind them of their success.

Some people mistakenly think politics endurable only for a
puritan who likes to show off. They see the politician as a person
exposed to the sight of all and held to the level of rectitude of
a schoolteacher in a small town or a man of the cloth, while
subject to derisive criticism which is even harder to take than the
insulting condescension accorded teachers and parsons. But in
fact the public insistence on observance of domestic moral rules
is not strict. Neither divorce nor the frequent commission of
adultery wins a politician any votes, but neither one is a crippling
handicap any longer, even for the highest positions, unless the
circumstances are openly scandalous. In such matters, most
voters condemn a politician not for private immorality but for
lowering the dignity of his office.

▼

The speech of politicians tends to be as drab as their sins. As
in politics, few men successful in the management of affairs in
private life have clear-cut individuality, and in each field their
character type tends to be uniform. A major reason which does
not apply to politicians is the increase in specialization. A man
bent on success would fall behind in his race if he were to spend
time learning things in many fields. He could not acquire more
than a superficial knowledge of each. Of course, it is a drawback
if one's knowledge and skill are narrower than the limits of the
job, and the limits do widen at each higher level. If in competition
in a narrow field a man can achieve enough superiority to rise
to the broader levels, then he can effectively employ what
broader outlook and knowledge he may have but did not use. Yet
even up there most of the world's knowledge is still outside.

Many of these able Americans in private life are dull in speech because their attention tends to be kept within the immediate limits of their work. Politics makes dull men but for a different cause. Burke said that the law sharpened a man's mind by making it narrow. Politicians' minds are rarely narrow but often flat. Most are full of fascinating experience. But a politician is inhibited by the hazards of his profession. Seldom are his comments on the world amusing or clear-cut. Distrustful even of an audience of friends because he knows that every sentence from his mouth may be taken some day by itself and used to harm him, he is bound to the formula for dullness: accuracy and completeness about details and vagueness about general ideas. His talk of facts is constricted to banality by his need to be correct. For the sale of stocks and bonds it is almost impossible to draft a prospectus in language which at the same time will be eloquent yet satisfy the SEC. Ogden Nash's poem contrasting accuracy and wit contains the line, "If it's right, it's trite." Yet when a politician gives his own opinions he shuns exactitude. His words have rounded edges for he knows he may be understood. Clarity is perilous unless transfigured by enchantment, a blend given only to those who speak with the melodic line of a Mozart. And even they dare not sing out for fear some unresolved chord will be plucked from the score and used against them. An ex-politician no longer fears to fascinate but often is too old to learn.

▼

For men who manage affairs in private life and for politicians as well, the daily life of incessant work toward a single goal tends to be the result of an egocentric nature and the cause of a dull one. On their way upward in a hurry, these men have no time for reflection or idle curiosity. Although some of their faculties are highly developed, they tend to be indistinct in personality. An important cause is the intensity of competition, partly due in turn to the horizontal and vertical extensions of opportunity—to choose one's vocation and to rise in it. Christopher Fry has Moses say, "The golden bear Success hugs a man close to its heart, and breaks his bones." Except for a few whose remarkable qualities enable them to retain their identities, politicians lose their sharp edges on the way to the summit, which is a table top covered with ivory billiard balls. Thomas Mann wrote: "In an age that affords no satisfying answer to the eternal question of 'Why?' 'To what end?' a man who is capable of achievement over and above the average and expected modicum must be equipped either with a moral remoteness and single-mindedness which is rare indeed and of heroic mould, or else with an exceptionally robust vitality."

▼

A man who wishes to excel as a lawyer should forswear politics. As in any other competitive field, an almost exclusive attention is essential both to pre-eminence and to first-rate performance. But for one to be competent in his practice, political activity is compatible, even congenial, with law. To look at this another way, if politics is his main interest, law is a good home base. Although this factor is overrated, a legal background is a help in the performance of a politician's job, because the work experience of a lawyer, even a specialist, covers such a wide variety of facts in his community. In a way, one is better prepared for politics by a background in business than by a background in law because business and political decisions both deal with possible future events, while arguments before a court look mainly to the past. Also, in appeal to voters, a background in small business probably ranks above one in law, which is a less popular profession in this century than it was in the last.

The practice of law is a castle which a man can leave for a venture in politics. When the fortunes of war or his own taste require, he can return to it more easily than to most other lines of work. "During my various excursions into public life," Henry Stimson once declared, "I always felt that I remained a lawyer with a law firm waiting as a home behind me, to which I could return on the completion of my public task and where I could always find awaiting me congenial friends and collaborators in the law."

And law is a worthy and satisfying alternative to politics. A man in public life can afford to take a more upright course if he is aware that his constituents lack the power to banish him to anything worse than the conditions of a lawyer's life.

▼

To use politics as a means to increase one's law practice is not very effective, although a fairly innocent motive. It makes a man well known but not in his capacity as a lawyer. If his political activity makes his practice flourish, he finds that he has ceased to practice law; he is retained not for his skill with the lawyer's tools of analysis, debate, and scholarship, but either for his "connections," whom he tries to persuade in matters where the official decision is to be made by standards which are mainly subjective, or for his knowledge of the maze through which he guides his masters. He is a salesman or a seeing eye. The only resemblance which his work bears to that of a lawyer is the title under his name on the office door.

Businessmen rarely get their money's worth from "influence" peddlers, who often sell them a bill of goods about how they know the passwords. Most people have as much success if they approach an official without an intercessor's help. To get an audience with a politician, no matter how august, you do not need to be his friend. High public officials are easier to approach than other busy men. It is no handicap that your closest contact with important politicians may be no more than a handshake with Kefauver or a signed picture from Ike.

Some lobbyists are paid a lot because they know important men and are thought to have their ear, but a lobbyist's power is less in those he knows than in those he represents. Few are like the Pope in having power without any armored divisions. The effective ones are those who marshal the things which influence politicians: vocal constituents, campaign contributors, and persuasive information about the matter to be decided. Without this leverage behind him, a lobbyist coaxes and appeals to old acquaintanceship in vain. He is known to be an agent for pay. A politician may yield to evidence, logic, temptation, or pressure, but he will not do much wrong to help the money-making of a friend.

The devices used to influence political decisions are spread across a moral spectrum. At one end are bribes and blackmail; dispassionate argument and information are at the other. As persons, the types range from criminals to upright citizens who exercise their right of petition to improve their government or to protect another right. The steps between are neither high-principled effort nor statutory crime. They include threats, promises, eloquence, entertainment, telegram avalanches, desk-pounding delegations and investment tips. Whether using them is a breach of civic duty or whether yielding to them is abuse of public trust depends on the degree of three things: the irrationality and force of the methods; their use by other contending parties so as to compel their adoption by all in order for each to hold his own; and the existence of an objective standard by which the choice can be made in the public interest so that reasonable men can agree on a single course.

A government official who is hired by another person has been bribed to use his power against the public interest. If his power is real even though his position is private in form, like a party chairman, a different law applies, but the morals are the same. If, like Senator Bricker, his excuse for his retainers from a railroad is his sincere belief in railroads' right to preference in public policy, even if he is telling the truth he still forgoes the right to change his mind. On the other hand, he cheats his customers if, like Lord Chancellor Francis Bacon, he takes money and then does the right thing or, if the matter is one of opinion, follows his own best judgment.

▼

To enter politics costs a person little in his vocational progress. The return is the rub. The likelihood that they cannot recover their former private stations deters many good men from a whirl at politics. On returning, a person tends to be set back further in his private career than if his time away from it had been spent in some neutral occupation such as the armed forces, although not as far as if he had been in jail.

He may have to enter some new line of work. Doors are slammed shut behind one who undertakes elective public service. It is feared that a teacher might corrupt the youth with evil mysteries which have been revealed to him. A man employed in business loses caste but usually is allowed to return so long as he has not opposed his employer's interests or contradicted his beliefs. A lawyer always can resume his practice, but he, too, is set back. Some people assume that he lacks judgment, or that his practice was so poor he ran for office in order to better himself. Others fear to entrust their substantial affairs to a man who may be orating on a platform instead of tending to business. In the time spent away from practice he falls behind his colleagues in attainment of learning and skill. Perhaps lawyers suffer less blame than others for entering politics because some people do not expect any more of them. The prospect of the stony ground on which a politician tends to fall when he returns to private life keeps some inferior men in politics at the same time that it keeps good men out.

Although it is well for the roles of citizen and politician to differ in texture and color so that each man may better know who he is, the transition between should not be hard. Except by change in public attitude there does not seem to be a way to lower the wall that impedes the healthy tidal flow between politics and private life. For three reasons a smaller sacrifice should be exacted from a man when he comes back from politics: Good men are encouraged to enter politics if the price to them on departure from it is not so high; politicians more easily can be righteous if the cost of defeat is lower; and they more easily can be wise if they are sometimes out of politics.

A permanent career service in elective office, implied in the proposals for special training of prospective politicians, is impossible under our electoral system. It is also undesirable, as shown by the examples of England and, even more, of France. Not all the arguments for a permanent career apply as well to politics as to other work. After a time the public tires of a person who no longer has anything new to tell or give them. Perhaps this is right and not to be regretted. Since a man's effectiveness as a teacher and guide depends partly on his personality and approach to life, his power to contribute may be reduced after he has performed before the same audience for long. A politician's assets include outlook and character, as well as training and experience. Few men retain enough perspective without recurrent periods in private life. During the height of his career as chief of Israel, Ben Gurion left office to this end for a year on a farm. Theodosius did the same, to save skin rather than soul, until he was called to lead and rule the Roman Empire. Tiberius, probably for motives more narrowly ambitious, secluded himself for seven years just before he reached the top.

▼

For the purpose of this book it will be enough to define freedom as the widest possible range of choice for each person through each moment of time. A more penetrating definition would add nothing here. As Fats Waller said to the young lady who asked him to define swing music, "If you gotta ask, you ain't got it."

A politician may try to make a free society as either a liberal or a conservative, whose doctrines are opposite sides of the same coin, like those of Jefferson and Hamilton. Without liberty, an orderly society can be stagnant and unanimous but not stable or harmonious. As an end in itself, order is futile and security ignoble, although both are indispensable conditions to political liberty which, in turn, is an essential means to a society of free men. It should not be forgotten that this, too, is not a final end, but it does no harm for politicians to treat it as one. Liberals and conservatives differ in emphasis only. They stand together against those who prefer the swerving road between tyranny and chaos. One's choice, liberal or conservative, depends on the shape of one's outlook and the needs of the time. As the latter may change, so, like Halifax, may a politician shift his own position if the liberal and conservative outlooks are blended in him. It is harder to do this where party boundaries are mainly ideological, so that a shift means a change of party, than it is in the United States, where at any given moment each party contains among its members almost every currently held political belief.

▼

What are the rewards of this profession? It gives the pleasure of dealing with people, the fascination of work with ideas, the challenge of problems important to all the world, and the satisfaction of fulfilling a central function of human society. At a time and place more harsh than here today, Achad Haam declared:

"I live for the perpetuation and happiness of the community of which I am a member; I die to make room for new individuals who will mold the community afresh and not allow it to stagnate and remain forever in one position. When the individual thus values the community as his own life and strives after its happiness as though it were his individual well-being, he finds satisfaction and no longer feels so keenly the bitterness of his individual existence, because he sees the end for which he lives and suffers."

A politician of many years tends to find private life unsatisfying. Even after circumstances isolate him, his ties to politics remain intact. Few can retire and, like Diocletian or Garner, find their gardens more diverting. Politics holds the attention of most veterans to the end. Not until six months before Andrew Jackson died at seventy-eight did he feel that he could write a friend, "I can now say in truth like Simeon of old, 'Now let thy servant depart in peace' "—and even then he was rejoicing at the election of Polk.

▼

2

MOTIVES AND INCENTIVES

Men and women are drawn into politics by a combination of motives; these include power, glory, zeal for contention or success, duty, hate, oblivion, hero worship, curiosity, and enjoyment of the work. Each motive is provoked by the incentive of some corresponding aspect or condition of politics. In most cases, the incentive is the mere general opportunity to satisfy the motive. For example, to a person wishing a test of his own capacity the structures of politics may be like mountaintops to a climber. But in some cases a specific thing is an incentive. A person in whom the motive of the public good was first perhaps implanted by family tradition or by reading lives of great men may be inspired to action by some current issue that stirs him. Another, like James Fenimore Cooper, whose reading of a worthless novel provoked him to quit his work and write a good one, may decide that he can, and therefore should, give a better performance than that of some official whose performance appalls him.

Each change in social relationships has been followed by a resulting change in moral obligations. The master-servant relationship imposed the duty of loyalty up and down. A century ago, Sir Henry Maine wrote, "The society of our day is mainly distinguished from that of preceding generations by the largeness of the sphere which is occupied in it by Contract." The contractual relationship exacted the duty to keep one's word. Now, the individual's relation to others, and his moral duty as well, are being shifted toward larger groups, primarily the community or state, and away from other individuals. Good citizenship in its broad meaning has become a primary moral duty, and politics its largest means of fulfillment. Politicians are assigned a major share of the function of turning to the better the strong forces, physical and social, which are at large. So much for duty.

The questions placed before politicians today challenge the intellect and inspire patriotic effort: the weapons of mass destruction; a continental economy which must at the same time be kept steady, made to produce and distribute, and allowed to experiment; the protection of individual freedom in an urban society as the organized groups which set and enforce the rules for behavior grow ever larger and more interdependent; the world-wide revolution, imposing on citizens the duty to keep their country safe while improving social justice overseas.

The whirlpool of politics offers oblivion to some. As part of changing crowds, one is absorbed in varied and incessant activity, never compelled, and seldom allowed, to sit still and expose one's mind to fundamental thoughts. Physicists think matter, and mind as well, to be an insubstantial swarm of related events, and so to knowing eyes the universe looks like air over the railroad tracks on a hot day. To those with little comprehension and perspective, who are not bound by an explanatory dogma, politics resembles this phenomenon. One also can reach oblivion unaccompanied, through meditation, drink, drugs, or a catatonic trance. Granted the longing to escape one's self, the choice of means is a matter of taste, and politics appeals to those who prefer flight in company of a sort. Politics does not attract those people who wish to hold on to themselves yet find that politics jostles them off balance. The unrelenting scramble to reach and hold office gives many of them, as well as those who tire of the chase, a longing for the refuge of the bench.

▼

Others enter the profession because it provides them with a medium through which to pursue a philosophy of conduct. A man often starts with youthful reflections about what he should make the purpose of his life. One who chooses politics may have a first-rate mind but rarely is a deep thinker about ultimates and almost never is trained in philosophy. He may have heard of Peirce or Wittgenstein, but the construction of his cosmos is likely to be an amateur job, helped by models from the ancients. He may hypothesize that his object is to do God's will, but his ignorance of this will leaves him where he started.

Is the world a moral gymnasium in which everyone should spend his life in the vigorous exercise of high principle so that mankind one day may constitute a sort of moral Olympic team? If he decides that man is perfectible, he begs the question again, because what do we do when all of us have become angelic toward God and each other? Does the earth become a monastery? How does a band of angels fill each day? Where pain and evil are abolished there is no work for the good. What if he decides that evil is here to stay? That limits our powers but leaves us with a choice of ends. If he expects eternal struggle and failure, for what should he work and fight? If he decides our proper goal to be an unattainable City of God, he still does not know what such a commonwealth is like nor even how to use his powers to establish morality, as distinguished from socially well-adjusted people's conduct, which tends to be what we regard as right.

Should he try to bring to pass a static world of cultivated materialists, who differ from the Polynesians only by being educated? Is it enough to supplement a life of eating bananas, playing the guitar, and going swimming, by providing each man with a foreign car, a tailored suit, a taste for good music, and a habit of tipping his hat to ladies? Is the graceful use of leisure man's proper end? If exclusive, is it even a satisfying end? Now that we are becoming free to consume much of our lives in pursuit of our pleasures we discover that they pall far sooner than Andrew Marvell expected when he told his coy mistress that if only they had infinite time he would enjoy spending a century in praise of her eyes and forehead before he went on to other things. Is a

life of elevated play redeemed by the fact that everyone is mo-
nogamous and temperate, has a Ph.D., goes to church and believes in the dignity of man? The notion of such a low target is
repellent. Man's aspiring nature enables him to fly upward, but
where and for what? Even on pragmatic grounds alone, the dis-
covery of new ends is called for now because without them few
people can be content.

The human race is on its way to join the leisure class. As a
Tibetan Buddhist whacks a prayer wheel without breaking stride,
soon one may supply his daily material needs with brief and casual effort. It is time to consider, if not yet to decide, how to use
our leisure. We can have aimless flight from boredom or a variety
of utopias. What are we free to do in our pursuit of happiness?
Create Beauty and search for the Truth. If he has no gift for
either, a youth may enter politics to make a society which permits others to do both.

▼

Politics offers more incentive when goals of policy can be seen
and are approached. The periods of consolidation tend to be less
tempting than the periods of advance. In the middle 1930's, although the means were in dispute and were matters of experiment, the general aims, such as protection of investors from
business deceit and the end of mass unemployment and wide
disparity of wealth, were stars by which to steer. These no longer
show the way. The problems of that time have been solved, have
diminished, or have passed away. For a long time thereafter they
were talked about as though they still existed; to end our troubles
we were urged merely to redouble the force with which we applied
old tools such as deficit spending, easy credit, and giving organized
labor a helping hand. The new problems have hardly yet been
recognized as the first step toward their mastery.

Especially during slack times, some people prefer to discern
problems and shape long-range goals. For this they must sit on
the bank of the stream. They cannot be politicians too. A politi-

cian is not only without honor in his own land but he is not a prophet at all. He learns his lessons from the prophets, whose sights are farther ahead. He is too busy with current emergencies to chart the stars, although he can follow them. He is a pilot, not a navigator.

There is a stronger incentive to jump into the fray when the two major parties are sharply divided by issues. The parties' paths diverge, converge, and sometimes even cross. When they are almost tweedledum and tweedledee, about the only persons to enlist are those who are more interested in organization than in issues, or those of combative temper who enjoy war for its own sake. A prospective politician may look at the parties as Buridan's ass looked at the two bales of hay.

A clear-cut division recruits not only more politicians but better ones. The public interest is served by having good men and women in both parties, but it is harmed by persons who enter politics without caring which party they join. An inconspicuous danger is those men of common sense whose policies are neither guided nor distorted by philosophies of government. Unless a politician believes in some of the stands he takes he is almost sure to follow a wavering line of expedience. A politician with some direction of his own tends to attract others of his kind because he keeps the parties apart. The outs look for, and in this case easily find, reasons to disagree with the ins. But where the ins are led by men who stand for everything and nothing there is little with which the outs can join issue, and so the parties converge.

Some young people choose to join a party which has many members in office. They like to be identified with a winning team and enjoy the warmth radiating from those in power. When they go to meetings, instead of adopting peevish resolutions criticizing the current leadership they hear first-hand reports of meals at the White House and almost classified matters of great import.

Others have an investor's approach. Like Caesar, who joined the broken faction of Marius, they prefer to enter a party at a low point so they can ride up with it. Where a party is weak and small a new arrival may be welcomed with hospitality. His recognition will be quicker and his apprenticeship shorter than where the ranks are crowded and places of responsibility are more sought after and more tightly held.

To some people politics offers a better opportunity for success than they have in other vocations which may attract them. This incentive applies to many women and also, in a declining degree, to those men, such as Truman, whose formal education is unequal to their abilities. It applies as well to those people whose background of training for some other vocation is second-rate. Graduates of obscure professional schools are more likely to enter politics than are those from the leading schools because in politics their undistinguished formal training is not only not held against them but may be an advantage. The fact that their kind of school experience is common to more voters gives these persons more appeal.

There are so many men of low ability in politics that it sometimes looks like a struggle between the one-eyed and the blind. This condition deters those with discriminating taste, while it attracts the ambitious who hope to take advantage of soft competition. On the other hand, the presence in politics of men able to climb high but likely to do harm repels the squeamish, while it inspires idealists to battle. In the past a common dangerous type has been the fanatic with a mind like a locomotive who is willing to stamp on whoever might stand in his way. A menace now is not a dark, unrelenting oppressor but a decisive weather vane, who measures the wind's direction, then bolts headlong that way to run interference for his constituents; he is a warm and shiny salesman who rehearses his sincerity before a mirror every morning and burns a candle to opinion polls each night.

The quality and congeniality of the company in politics are a stronger incentive or deterrent than when there were more self-willed men who knew where they wanted to go and did not pay much attention to the scenery on the way. A rise in average levels of quality and ability among politicians tends to invite more people than it discourages.

Prosperity works both ways. Easy living makes people less willing to submit to the hard grind of politics. Yet easier fulfillment both of obligations for family support and of the need for self-support enables men to enter politics who otherwise would feel they could not afford it. Prosperity's effects on prospective politicians and young athletes are alike, deterring some from turning professional and enabling others to take part as amateurs.

▼

When ready to retire, some men run for office to obtain a final adornment to a successful career in business or a profession or to pay a debt to the community in which they have flourished. But regardless of such a man's motives, whether generous or immature, unless he enjoys the daily work itself his performance will disappoint his constituents and his experience will disappoint him.

A candidate for county commissioner told me that his motive was "prestige" in the community of which he was the leading disk jockey. By the change in employment he stood to become less widely known and far less popular. Yet he wanted the job so much that he shaved his beard.

▼

A voter's motive is thought to be negative more often than affirmative. Yet many people are lured into political activity for the first time by enthusiasm for a politician whom they admire, while a comparative few start with a purpose of inflicting a defeat. On the other hand, this may be the sole motive of a person who files once again for office after having been rejected by the people and licked by an opponent. Those in a similar position who are less consumed by a thirst for revenge or a need to prove or justify themselves are able to stay in private life because they know that for one who returns to politics with no other purpose than this,

"The pleasure is momentary, the position ridiculous and the expense damnable."

▼

For centuries young men have bounded into politics, fired by Plutarch to play some heroic part in their country's history. Euripides wrote:

"Thou hast heard men scorn thy city, call her wild
Of counsel, mad; thou hast seen the fire of morn
Flash from her eyes in answer to their scorn!
Come toil on toil, 'tis this that makes her grand,
Peril on peril! And common states that stand
In caution, twilight cities, dimly wise——
Ye know them, for no light is in their eyes!
Go forth, my son, and help!"

However, as the opportunities to rise in other ways have expanded, the chances for glory have contracted. As objects of worship, God and man together have gone down. Heroes tend less to be adored or even recognized as such. With a general equality of comforts, the need for vicarious living is lessened, and with the diminishing attribution of personal responsibility sainthood is abolished along with sin. Especially in politics and war, glory's value has become hardly worth its price.

War's increasing destructiveness has narrowed its utility as a policy. War's increasing specialization and collective organization have made the soldier's profession less glorious. For other reasons, the utility of politics has been enlarged, while the glory of political leadership has suffered a corresponding decline. Power has been diffused so that there is less of it to go with the glory. It has become harder to hold a conspicuous place in the direction of affairs, both public and private, but more so in government because the leaders are more vulnerable. (In big business, where men on top enjoy a hidden eminence, the main incentive to rise has been shifted, by taxes on income and estate transfers, from wealth to renown within the ranks.) Some persons deny that any superiority exists in order that their own may not arouse envy. The crowd's resentment of the heads that show above it makes ambitious men try for concealed power and let the glory go. One who would serve his community must do so by short and patient steps to bring about slow change. No longer can he step out before his city like Hector or Horatius and strike decisive blows. He who wants to be a hero has a better chance in the fields of entertainment and sport.

Often public life suggests to onlookers the splendor and simplicity of grand opera. But a politician feels more like one member of a big orchestra which is improvising with intricate subtlety. He is absorbed in unheroic detail. A French politician, tormented by inroads of American culture and Algerian arms, may regret that it would be no use for him to strap his harness on his back, rise up like Roland, resolute before the Saracen host, and sword in hand call out, "Praise God and all His holy angels, France shall never lose her name through me!"

▼

Many men enter politics because they want to be the center of attention. Self-preoccupied, they may not always boast, but in conversation refer everything to themselves. Such a man often thinks of himself as an institution. In the past some of these have been successful demagogues, but their kind is becoming extinct along with the backwardness of the regions in which they prospered. Not many of them now go far. Some never win an election. Others drop out after a short time. A few have intelligence enough to discover their handicap and enough ambition and capacity for growth to subdue it.

Many successful politicians have an equally narrow but more sophisticated selfishness. Subordinating the present gratification of their pride to long-run fulfillment of their self-serving aims, sacrificing vanity to ambition, they forgo immediate praise for the sake of rapid self-advancement. Instead of talking about himself such a politician flatters others to get his way, never letting his ego impede its own eventual success.

In degree of pride politicians range between two extremes: At one end there are haughty men who are concerned with government for, but not by, the people and whose paternalistic attitude is often a mask for class prejudice; at the other extreme are those who imitate and grovel. As times have grown more democratic, the mid-point has moved toward the sedulous apes. No living politicians resemble Coriolanus, who generated resentment even in his day by a proud and stubborn temper that put the public interest below his ego, and who insulted people in the effort to avoid debasing himself by flattering them. Woodrow Wilson, who stood about as far on that side of the middle as any successful American politician in this century, wrote in 1884, "I have a sense of power in dealing with men collectively which I do not feel always in dealing with them singly. In the former case the pride of reserve does not stand so much in my way as it does in the latter. One feels no sacrifice of pride necessary in courting the favour of an assembly of men such as he would have to make in seeking to please one man." One doubts that he would succeed as well today.

▼

Politics is an all-or-nothing venture that does not easily fit into the scheme of a person who enters it to fulfill part of an aim which is wide rather than high. Such a person proposes to cover the same units of area but on a broad front rather than a long ladder. He may wish to do fairly well in several fields at once: for example, to be skilled in his profession, to do his duties as a parent and a citizen, and to become a gentleman and a scholar. He would rather excel in the decathlon than in a single event. But most of his political rivals prefer to excel in politics alone. He rarely rises far in politics, not only because he gives it part time in competition with others who give it all their time, but also because he is not competing as hard in the total of his pursuits. He puts out less intense effort because he is not surrounded by persons competing on his own terms for the same goals and because he does not have models of his own kind of success for him to emulate. He is perplexed with continual decisions, wondering when to leave his office for work on some civic or domestic function. For the persons with a single-field ambition, there are dramatic examples of their kind of success, like Alexander's monument before which Caesar wept in Spain.

If this diffused ambition, now growing more common, should become widely held, it would be less of a handicap in competition for supremacy in a single field because there would be a smaller proportion of single-field competitors. Yet, at the same time, if this outlook should be held for long by a substantial number of persons, heroic models would be established by those who had achieved such a combination goal. Both their presence, and the new subscribers whom they tended to attract, would stiffen competition for this cluster of aims.

▼

Some stay in politics because they like the work. Gregarious, energetic, internally secure, they enjoy the attention and acclaim and do not mind the knocks. Children, debts, and other hostages to fortune do not trouble those to whom the stony road of politics is like the brier patch to Br'er Rabbit.

▼

3

LIABILITIES

One who enters politics must realize that he is to live dangerously. In business, the line between the red and the black divides anxiety and comfort, but a businessman can survive a bad year; in politics .1 per cent of one's biennial gross vote can mean the difference between prosperity and ruin. Some politicians would say it is the difference between anxiety and ruin.

Between politics and other professions runs a deep crack. At the bottom are a lot of nice fellows. A defeated candidate, conscious of this hazard, often resumes his former work with desperation rather than enthusiasm as he hustles to make up for lost time.

For a man of active intellect the most severe condition of politics is to abstain from the full and constant use of his powers. He must be willing to submit to boredom and make the effort to conceal it. Insofar as a politician works in his party organization his patience is taxed by tedium such as service on committees engaged in administration (e.g., organizing a dinner meeting or picnic), a function suited to a single person. Most political meetings are dull enough to spur the ambition of impatient men. By custom, a private has to sit through them in silence, an officer is allowed to speak, and a general may arrive at the end to make the main oration during which he may while away the time by listening to his own voice.

To converse on public affairs is often stimulating. To compose a speech on some important issue is satisfying. To deliver it sometimes is exhilarating. Those occasions on which one is able to entertain or amuse a responsive audience are great fun. But much of the public relations work, in and out of campaigns, is a pattern of sitting through long meetings where the business transacted and the ceremonies performed are almost identical with what took place at the meeting the evening before, which was dull the first time; then at the end, one must circulate within the group as it breaks up and greet strangers or acquaintances with a cordial handshake. Politics, like parenthood, is less paternal than it used to be, but it resembles parenthood in the drudgery which is a part of both.

In politics, the rate of pay is modest, although not as low as one might think from the complaints of some. Expense is high and much is not tax deductible. Because, unlike happiness, money-making can be best achieved by direct approach, politics is no place for anyone who wants to make big money, or, unless he has it already, to live on a scale of comfort which requires it. The main loss of income caused by politics is not the drop, if any, in actual net income on entering public office. It is rather that following a period of political activity the long-run level of private income tends to be below what it would have been if the person had stayed where he was and polished the handle of the big front door. Although having done time in politics is likely to reduce a person's total lifetime income, this loss, because evenly spread and deferred to future years, is a weaker deterrent than the conditions, say, of becoming a physician, where the austerity comes at the start.

Some other lines of work take as much effort, but, except for some kinds of medical practice, none allows less time free from the cares of the job. The hours are too irregular and long to permit a satisfactory family life, although extensive political activity can be postponed until the children are of such an age that no one suffers much from your absence except your wife. After sundown far from home a politician may remind himself that "I have promises to keep, and miles to go before I sleep."

Cirrhosis of the liver has been called an occupational disease of newspapermen, and the same could be said of politicians. Drinking often becomes a problem because of long meetings and conferences under conditions which encourage it, in hotels, lodge halls, restaurants, and homes. Social conventions permit it, and exacting thought is not required. Artificial aid seems almost imperative to men who feel they must be as genial as Santa Claus in conversation with the fiftieth stranger they have met that day. It is hard not to tire of playing the cheery friend to all the world and the devoted slave of one's constituents. But in this profession are some teetotalers and few drunkards, because ambition is to politics what hope of profit is to business, and it is strong enough in most politicians to protect them from the allurements of drink.

▼

It would be less perplexing to be a politician if one did not have to learn to make, and practice making, a living in two ways, as a politician and in some private work. In order to live, and also to acquire the respected status which will help him to be elected, he must apply much of his time to acquiring knowledge and practicing skills not directly connected with public affairs, and which may not be easy for him or of special interest to him. For success in most lines of work, a person's choices of activity in other, unconnected fields and his failures or successes in them are irrelevant. A physician's practice is not impaired by the fact that stocks always drop as soon as he buys them, nor is it assisted by the fact that he is a renowned poet. But a politician is measured to some extent by the nature and quality of his work performance outside politics. In politics, as elsewhere, nothing succeeds like success, but success in another field is often a condition to making a successful jump from private to public life.

A politician is helped or hurt in politics by both the choice of his private work activity and the level of his private success, which has less effect on his political success than does the nature of the private work itself. He may be shunned as unsound if he is known as an artist, good or bad, and some voters may doubt his interest in the public welfare if he has shown himself to be a gifted speculator, no matter how legitimate. For him to excel in certain fields may handicap him more than if he failed. Having gone broke as a storekeeper did not cost Lincoln or Truman many votes, but either man might have found it hard to reach the White House through the needle's eye of the Board Chairmanship of Montgomery Ward.

In many constituencies it tends to be harder to acquire the public respect and confidence necessary for election if one does not wear the mantle of the man of affairs. Some people suspect the ideas and proposals of one who does not accept tradesmen's values. Having "met a payroll" has lost some of its appeal, but long-sustained effort in the management of affairs continues to be an important asset in earning the respect of one's fellow men. Some teachers who enter politics surmount this handicap by superior knowledge of the subject matter in politics and by skill in presenting it to their audience. However, some experience acquired in the management of affairs is not merely relevant to questions of public policy but is an essential condition to political competence. Also, because a person's political ideas or abilities to apply them may be worthless, the practice of his private profession can serve as a useful end and a safe hedge to the bets on which part of his life is committed.

Because life is too short for him to master two trades, a politician sometimes learns little more about public office than how to attain it, like a student who fails to get an education because he concentrates on grades to keep his scholarship. Few men are frustrated for long by this thinly spread application of their time. Most either do not mind it, become resigned to it, or quit. Even if a politician's main interest is politics, so long as he enjoys people and the busy life of affairs, in or out of government, he is not much discontented by the differences in subject matter between his public and private callings. Also, if he prefers politically unacceptable work, this fact may prove to him and others his lack of fitness for politics.

▼

Mendes-France said, "To govern is to choose," but a politician's choices give offense. He does not coldly call them as he sees them. No one thinks him a mechanism which makes automatic choices as an agent of the Law, a brooding presence overhead. Everyone knows he cares about his decisions. As both referee and advocate, he plays in a game for which he makes the rules, and the rules are the object of the game. He is less protected than unknown umpires or majestic, impersonal judges. Seldom are more than a few people at a time hurt by the ruling of a trial court, but a strong, revengeful group is ready for ignition by a governor's appointment or a legislator's vote. Because a politician estranges many people by what he does or fails to do, popularity, in contrast to notoriety or fame, is not as easy to attain or to keep in politics as in some other fields, although many politicians have a craving to be liked.

When public opinion about a policy issue is widely held and strongly in contradiction to what a politician thinks is wise or just, he has to yield in principle or power. He must choose between declining to run at the next election, conforming to the public wish, or disregarding the sentiment and inviting defeat. Like an actress asking a casting director for a part, his response to these distasteful conditions depends on the comparative pulls on him of his principles, his ambition, and his taste. The most public-spirited citizen has the right, sometimes the duty, to say for himself, "The public opinion be damned." But even if at times a politician does not follow public opinion he always must give it respect.

▼

Another hazard, less real than apparent, is the restraint on free speech. The argument goes like this: On most jobs your speech must be circumspect in the presence of employer, clients, and customers, but after work you may say what you please; a servant of the public, however, whether actual or aspirant, never can escape the agents of his employer; such continual discretion is an inconvenience requiring severe discipline until it becomes a habit. This overstates the difference between the speaking conditions of public and private life. The practical limits on unpopular speech are similar for a politician and any private person whose position is a responsible one in the conduct of affairs. A man's associations often compel him to be silent so as not to hurt others close to him in his business or his firm. The silence of business life is more absolute than the cautious reticence of politics. In general, compared with private life speech in politics is less free for casual conversation, yet more free for issues. A politician may feel he should refrain from complaining to a friend at lunch about the cost of haircuts because this remark might start a rumor that he is "against the barbers"; yet without disloyalty to his associates he can lead a street march for one side of a disputed issue, while if he were not in public life he might feel ashamed to appear at his place of work the morning after such a performance.

To be a brave and useful politician it is not necessary to speak out boldly whenever you differ from your associates or party. Political ties have their loyalties, and there are occasions when a man must keep silent, or else blunt the thrusting edge of his convictions. Here comes the time for anxious study and balancing what is to be gained by speaking out as against waiting his turn. Without sacrifice of the public interest, a compromise can be struck between saying nothing about anything and letting the chips fly. A man's duty demands candor, while his survival demands discretion. As much as possible, a politician must refrain from criticism of individuals and groups, except by inference; such talk is the main source of antagonisms. The public interest does not obligate him to make truthful statements about the truthfulness of used car dealers or Hearst newspaper editors. When asked about a pending issue, he has the duty to speak out clear and straight. But one may mitigate the rancor of those who feel the other way by phrasing one's declaration in terms which accommodate the audience. General answers of opinion are more likely to inflame than specific answers of fact. Arguing the merits of a specific solution to a problem is safer than asserting controversial principles, which may antagonize whether understood or misunderstood, and more useful than asserting principles on which everyone agrees.

Speech in politics is on the whole as free as it is in at least some important walks of private life, and thought is more free. Of late we have been learning the falsity of the old assumption that everyone is unfettered in his thoughts, no matter what restrictions may be imposed on his rights to express them. Russia and China have shown by extreme examples that conditions imposed on the individual not only can silence him but can cramp his thinking as well. The practice is to invade his thoughts, compel him to chant a litany, and then when this becomes a routine so that he can ignore it, he is made to declare some new belief. No longer can a person under such conditions reassure himself that "Come what may, I shall be undisputed master in the castle of my skin." Although the forces operating on Americans in private life are weaker and less calculated, our private citizens often become so molded by their work that after five o'clock they think and speak the way they do while on the job. In 1940, an advertisement appeared in the Chicago *Tribune* declaring that: "In a last stand for democracy, every director and officer of this bank will vote for Wendell Willkie." Those labor union spokesmen who for a long time claimed that the Taft-Hartley Act had repealed the Thirteenth Amendment did not exemplify such frozen thought only because most of them either did not believe what they said or erred from lack of knowledge; they were demagogues or ignorant, but not true believers.

A businessman, conformed by his eagerness for money, recognition, or power, becomes as empty as his counterpart in public life. Even more so, because in many walks of private life thought is numbed by the pursuit of money, while in politics the strife, in part, is over ideas. The habit of expressing ideas, even if not one's own, is a help. Most conversations in which a politician takes part are the same as those of other people, confined to small talk, big talk, and shop talk. Among politicians, talk is often gossip, but despite the limits on their jurisdiction, the subject matter of their conversations with other people has an almost unlimited range.

▼

It is no harder for a politician than for a private person to stand up for principle. In politics this action tends to be taken before a crowd. There a speaker's feelings may remain more protected within himself than when he confronts another individual, the more common situation in private life. Political communication's current shift from public meetings to the media makes even more impersonal the atmosphere in which a politician declares a position which may please or offend. His thinking can be more independent of the audience, more concentrated on the subject matter, when he is looking at a camera lens or speaking to a mike. Face to face with another person, you are exposed to his reaction to you as a person. A crowd, visible or invisible, may do you harm or help you, but it will not scowl or smile.

The actual choice of side on an issue is as perplexing for a politician as for a private person, and when the side is publicly taken the exposure to criticism is the same whether one is in or out of public life. But the decision to take a stand at all, preliminary to the decision of what stand to take, is easier for a politician than for a private person because by doing nothing a politician cannot escape criticism or shame. Like a driver approaching a fork in the road, he knows that if he falters cars behind will honk. The burden of effort to get up from the armchair or bed and start action is lighter for a politician; he cannot succumb to inertia; he is jarred loose from his resting place.

When a private person sees a hot public issue he can stay in the shadows without disapproval. Even when asked, the private man can safely say, "I pass," while politicians must explain their indecision. If they fail to fulfill their publicly recognized duty to

take a position on important issues they suffer the consequences
of showing themselves evasive or weak. They cannot excuse themselves by ignorance, either admitted or claimed. If they do not
meet an issue they must pretend illness or claim that the issue
does not exist. Frequent visits to the hospital are impractical, and
it is uncomfortable to be scorned by both sides of a controversy
for dodging it. Therefore, the decision to take a public stand on
an issue requires less effort of a politician than of private persons,
who are not goaded into action and who have little to lose by
standing pat.

▼

A politician is exposed to abuse by opponents, critics, and constituents. Anyone is free to attack him and his family with falsehood or with painful truth, and many do. The half-truth is a
common device because of the low risk of either legal liability
or public disapproval of the author. Some news reports of a campaign resemble the ship's log in which, after the mate had written,
"Today the captain was drunk," the captain wrote, "Today the
mate was sober."

There are two forms of assault: on a politician's principles or
policies, and on his character. A man who calls for a tariff cut on
certain goods is damned by their local producers as an assassin
and a cad. It is not hard to get used to invective, just as a surgeon
gets used to the flow of blood. A politician is consoled by the
belief that he is right and that some others agree with him.
Abuse based on the things he stands for is faced without concern
by any sensible politician as a hazard of his job. After a local
convention, I saw a leading member of the U. S. Senate pushed
backward across a hotel lobby by a drunk who prodded him with
one thumb and dropped cigar ashes on his tie while scolding him
for his vote on a measure which had affected a commercial interest. The Senator kept repeating gently that he certainly respected the man's opinion. At last he backed into an elevator
which lifted him to a room filled with loyal adherents and smoke,
where he could expect to be put upon again.

In the other form of attack, no matter how preposterous the charges may be, lies about a politician's character upset and embitter him if their nature so combines with the climate of the time as to make some of his fellow men accept them as true. Even for a veteran the pain remains acute. He has no defense, he cannot prove his innocence; and there is no fair way to hit back except by ridicule, such as for example, Franklin Roosevelt's taunts at "Martin, Barton and Fish" and his defense of his "little dog Fala." But ridicule is effective only when the audience is not too distrustful, and it is available only to politicians with enough wit and commanding presence to put across their gay contempt.

An impersonal attitude toward personal attacks reduces the shock and helps a politician to react with more calm than a layman would, just as an athlete is not depressed or offended by bumps he takes from other players in the course of a game. At a Senate Committee hearing a certain McCarthy told a cruel lie about the young colleague of a lawyer named Welch, whom he thereby drove to tears, although Welch had a cool head and long experience in courts. Not even such a thing as this would make many politicians cry. However, players in a body-contact sport need only keep in mind that their opponents feel no spite, while a politician must try, not to remember but to ignore a fact, that his assailants often mean their blows to hurt; and therefore his defenses can be pierced.

To a politician whose policies follow the middle of the political road, abuse is like a wind blowing across it. He may move to the position opposite his critic, drifting over to the lee side for refuge and a kind word, or else going there in anger like the man who took the pitcher to the cellar for his wife. After he tripped on the top step and tumbled to the floor below, his wife called down, "Did you break the pitcher?" "No," he replied with an oath, "but I'm going to break it now!" On the other hand, a politician with a keener sense of survival but no more courage may try to refute his accusers by moving to join them on the windward side of the road.

▼

Men shrink from politics because they can be ruined by enemies. Friends are trouble too. The truth is hidden from a politician to keep him cheerful, or twisted to make him a more fiercely aggressive campaigner. A license to cheat the public by deceiving its servants tends to be assumed by persons who are otherwise upright.

Friendship is difficult. A politician sees many people but few of them often and over a long period. He loses friends when he acts or speaks against their wishes or beliefs. His profession is small, and the turnover is high. Few among those of his companions who remain follow the pattern of his location as it shifts between home town, county seat, state capital, and Washington. He is like a professional baseball player who does not come home in the off season. Enduring friendship is difficult because "in the frequent jumble of political atoms, the hostile and the amicable ones often change places." A politician has few friends, and he is sure of hardly any except those he knew when he was still unknown. Yet loneliness is the fate of the well-differentiated man wherever he finds himself, save as it may be cushioned by family ties. Among lawyers there is more comradeship than in any other vocation, but fellowship is less than friendship. A man with a clear-cut personality is fairly sure to feel lonely, whenever he stops to think of it. In public life he may receive inspiring loyalty that goes far to justify his personal isolation. But along with heroism and hero worship, now less common and less strong, such loyalty is in decline.

A politician may be lonely but he cannot be alone. About public leadership Montaigne wrote: "Ambition is of all others the most contrary humor to solitude; glory and repose are things that cannot possibly inhabit in one and the same place." Some kinds of ambition permit solitude, but ambition for power and glory during life does not.

Because politics is urban, a politician may frequently praise, but seldom enjoy, nature's beauties. The only exception is a part-time politician like the farmer who goes to the legislature in winter. On a summer afternoon a politician may attend a lodge picnic at a lakeside park but he cannot walk on mountain heather nor stroll alone among the green and rolling furrowed hills of cultivated land.

▼

Recognition for accomplishment is passing and uncertain. "It's not what you've done, it's what you've done lately" (or probably will do). This political proverb describes a fact which is in the public interest though often disappointing to an individual, as it was to Churchill in 1945. Nor is full credit given for merit. Acts of generosity, conviction, or even courtesy, are discounted as done for political gain. In principle, the practice of virtue is as it is in private life. For external rewards one has to wait for heaven.

A politician may receive gratitude for his acts of public service and he may be pitied for his misfortunes. In politics both gratitude and pity vanish as quickly as these fleeting sentiments do when directed at some person in private life. The transience of gratitude is the same on the part of a politician as it is for others who feel it toward him—as any President knows when he appoints a judge. Pity toward politicians is more common than gratitude. Although it is almost never felt for a loser, pity is often felt for personal misfortunes unconnected with failure, such as a death in the family. This pity is genuine and, because the politician is so well known, is widespread. President Eisenhower's partially disabling illnesses increased his support from some voters as much as it reduced it from others. Because pity often is a substantial motivating force for votes, a politician is in luck if circumstances choose campaign time in which to do him harm.

▼

The risks of becoming a megalomaniac or a cynic are not like Scylla and Charybdis because one can succumb to both at once.

Thus a politician may think politics nonsense, and at the same time refer to himself in the third person. The altitude of some offices encourages delusions of grandeur which are latent in many of the men attracted to politics. A politician who plays the big shot in order to meet the expectations of some constituents runs the danger of coming to believe his own pretense. Sometimes encouraged by his wife, a man may dream that destiny has chosen him to legislate in marble halls. Others give less thought to whether their country's money is going to bear a graven image of their heads. A State Senator told me, "How I hate to see my name in the papers. It's always something bad. I could be re-elected forever if I could only stay out."

If a politician reveals a touch of cynicism, humbugs in a swarm embrace him. Like everyone, he sees the world through his experience, and these companions confirm his cynicism. The pressure to be cynical is strong, and the withering effect of cynicism is hard to resist. He can be lonely and thick-skinned and discreet, yet remain himself. If he becomes a cynic he is an altered man, and a hollow one. He can escape this penalty, however, if he takes care not to expect an improbable rate of progress or level of goodness, and if he does not lose his nerve.

Under the temptation and pressure to respond to popular wishes and beliefs a politician may become nothing but a suggestion box for pressure groups, like the Emperor Claudius, "who had neither partialities nor dislikes, but such as were suggested and dictated to him." This hazard has increased. The public will is stronger, and a politician need no longer fear that by obedience to it he may forfeit his colleagues' respect; many guiding rules have disappeared. A dreadful private evil of public life is this corruption of personality, which produces men who have lost their savor and are "neither fit for the land, nor yet for the dunghill."

There are two ways to listen to what is said to you: to consider the content of the statement, or to try to discern the mind of the speaker and determine what response would be most effective to achieve your wishes in respect to him. In conversation most people combine the two approaches, but, like those theorists of teaching method who advise, "Teach the child, not the subject," these faceless men ignore the meaning of the content except as related to the feelings of their listeners. The crowd plays Hamlet to such a man's Polonius, prodding him on to shift his interpretations to please them. An echo board with nothing of himself to give, he may be addressed in the scornful words of Conrad's captain to the outcast, "What is there in you to provoke?"

A man can lose his soul anywhere, of course. In politics there are two protections from this risk: One is a moderate ambition, enough to maintain one's effort and purpose; the other is an alternative trade as a hole card to remind the politician of a further chance for service in another worthy calling after his defeat.

▼

A politician has to keep his place. He will be found at fault if he is either undignified or arrogant. The former sin is venial, the latter cardinal. As Tacitus once pointed out, men tend to "scrutinize with keen eyes the recent elevation of their fellows, and to demand a temperate use of prosperity from none more rigorously than from those whom they have seen on a level with themselves." The quality of a politician's bearing is measured against the background of his rank. Arrogance in a coroner is dignity in a governor.

Egotism is increased by the sweet music of applause, but humility is also induced by the conditions of a politician's life: to be told off and have to beg his daily bread from face to face. A successful politician has a strong ego, but he lacks that kind of pride which inhibits him from asking for help.

▼

Sometimes men are driven back to private life by exasperation with their constituents. People often resent a politician for his failure to be both delicately responsive to public wishes and a self-sustaining leader who leads. He disappoints them if he is not at once a thistledown on the breeze and a game fish that swims upstream. Hiram Gill, a former waiter, was elected Mayor of Seattle on a closed-town platform. He kept his promise and was dismissed from office at the next election. He ran again on an open-town platform, was elected, kept this promise, and was again defeated. This confused Gill, who just wanted to be Mayor.

Another attitude which makes for disappointed citizens and exasperated politicians is people's dislike of a cocksure manner and their concurrent wish that a politician be sure he knows the answers, since they did not elect him to doubt and ponder. They want a humble messiah. To combine modesty and certainty is less contradictory than to join responsiveness and leadership but is nonetheless a difficult standard to meet. A politician also knows that many of his constituents wish him to perform the functions of his profession yet be "above politics," where Eisenhower tried to be and where they think Lincoln was. For a politician's personality still another aggravating paradox is the common wish that he be both subservient and dignified, that he run petty errands, and run them as though he were descending Sinai with tablets of stone.

Imperious negative demands by constituents, often opposed to each other, may discourage one who thinks of going into politics. These persons intimidate politicians and stifle their enterprise. Subdued by threats, politicians often stand pat in order to survive or else resort to "the usual substitute for wisdom in waiting for the folly of others." In dealing with one's supporters, and with other pressure groups, one could learn from the football coach who hoped his team would lose no more games than just enough to "keep the alumni sullen but not mutinous." Indifferent to anything beyond their single purpose, these bitter citizens are less offended by sins of omission than by one act which they regard as wrong, even though combined with a record of good deeds. Politicians well may say to one another, "Constituents do make cowards of us all," and tell their fellow citizens, "He that depends upon your favors swims with fins of lead."

▼

4

DILEMMAS

A politician must draw delicate moral lines. Canons of professional ethics might assist him. When he performs his function of shaping public policy by striking compromises between conflicting interests and opinions, or by resolving his equally conflicting loyalties, it is wrongly claimed that he is compromising principle (his own and others'), and therefore lacks it. A recognized code of conduct might reduce this disapproval and also help to guide him among his duties. If he knew his adherence to a set standard would not put him at a disadvantage with his rivals who had accepted the same duty, he would be encouraged to raise his standards of practice. The effect of such a code of conduct, like the effect of a minimum wage law on industrial competitors, might be as much to enable as to compel.

What should be the rule for evasive answers, or the one for unspoken lies? How far should a candidate be held accountable for defamatory rumors which his supporters start? What should be his attitude toward a low caliber running mate for whose selection he has had no responsibility except the remote one of membership in the same party? May he protect himself by displaying disapproval of the other man, or does duty to his party constrain him to pretend respect?

Should a politician accept help from contributors with dishonest motives? If he does, what does he owe them? They expect a pay-off and deserve a double cross. He can choose the latter only once. Few have the chance to handle this problem with dispatch and satisfaction as did a certain man in 1952. When he had been elected to the Senate he received predated checks from men who despised what he stood for and had supported his opponent, but wished to do business with Uncle Sam. Gracious letters of thanks were sent to the donors explaining that he could not use the money, since his bills were paid, but that he knew how devoted they were to his principles so he had endorsed their checks to his party's state committee.

In deciding whether to accept a contribution, should a candidate distinguish between a frank sort who states his conditions when he offers money and a discreet one who does not? That is, are express contracts worse than implied ones? In the latter class does it make a difference whether the candidate knows of the offeror's business interest in governmental favor, and whether it is present or prospective? Is it all right if there is no meeting of the minds? How long before a campaign or after it may money be accepted?

How should he respond to offers of institutional support from unions, chiropractor societies, trade associations, and other special interest groups? In most elections a substantial measure of such help must be obtained to win. Yet most such groups give assistance as their end of an assumed bargain. Some of them help without asking, then come around with a request.

How specific must his answers be, and how sincere? Voters share half the blame for politicians' being vague and windy gladhanders. May he declare as his opinion what reflects his own record and what he thinks to be the view of most of his constituents, yet in truth is not his own? May he give a truthful answer as to his intended course but a false explanation of the motives which determined it? On a certain issue if he sees a conflict between the public's wish and welfare and he decides to heed the wish, may he give the public welfare as the reason for the attitude he takes?

What must the office holder do when he finds himself a prisoner of his own supporters? They may be for him on principle because of his policies. If, on principle, he should change his policies in order to conform them to his change of mind, he may lose his supporters, who will believe that he has lost his principles.

How narrow must a special interest be, how far in contradiction to the general good, how strong the pressure from the group which represents it, to make submission to the group's request not obedience to the people's will, but acceptance of a bribe or flight from a threat?

How far may a politician deviate from the truth in unimportant things? Dishonesty about trifles is a dangerous habit because hard to keep within limits, but there it does no harm. Like other artists, a politician may be allowed a license to improve a tale. On the Chicago plane with the Massachusetts delegation to the 1956 Convention, James M. Curley told me that F.D.R. had betrayed him, that after he had uncovered the depths of the President's baseness he addressed him in the words that Cardinal Wolsey spoke "to Cromwell who had condemned him to death and then had come to visit him: 'If I had served my God as well as I had served my king [substitute Roosevelt], He would not have left me naked and helpless before mine enemies.' " Imagine the response of his Boston crowds when Curley would put himself in the place of a Cardinal defying Cromwell. About these same words are thought to have been spoken by Wolsey to his friend Thomas Cromwell, a ruthless agent and a remote collateral ancestor of Oliver who was born sixty-nine years after Wolsey's death.

In the day of rule by kings, a courtier had the duty to impart painful facts "without wounding the delicacy of a royal ear." In addressing his masters, a politician is called on to learn and exercise this art. How does he locate the range between the limits which duty and survival set? Unlike a courtier, except in urging the defeat of his incumbent opponent he does not have to advise his constituents to correct their mistakes or faults. He need tell them nothing irrelevant to the problems which confront them both. He would not have to inform a group of Irishmen that Saint

Patrick was an Englishman. The hard choices come where the
politician decides whether to tell citizens the fact, as it appears
to him, that a certain policy which they may authorize will hurt
them later on more than help them immediately. Most kinds of
fiscal responsibility illustrate this kind of bad-tasting truth. In
action, a politician has the duty to carry out the wishes of his
constituents as modified by his conscience and his judgment. But
in speech he has the duty to tell people the truth about public
affairs. A large proportion of big vote getters dispense sugar-
coated pills because so many people prefer happy-ending fairy
tales. In his choice of what to say, one of a politician's hardest
ethical efforts is resisting the urge to follow Marshall Field's
motto: "Give the lady what she wants."

How much of the truth should a politician withhold from his
constituents when its public knowledge would not make people
angry with him but in some way would cause them harm? When
should a politician let his constituents know facts the knowledge
of which would help the constituents make their basic decisions
of national policy, yet which would also give another nation's
hostile government advantage as against our own? Should an
economist's report predicting a depressed business condition be
released to the public if the politician reasonably expects that
public knowledge of this report would depress business conditions even more than the report predicted? When is making this
kind of statement like screaming "Fire!" in a crowded theater—in
which there is in fact a fire? And when is withholding it an un-
justified treatment of citizens as children who must be sheltered
from facts which would confuse or hurt them? Politicians must
balance the harm which disclosure might cause against the advantage of the citizens' right, and free government's necessity to
have the whole truth in order to govern well. By pretending that
their duty to provide the whole truth is absolute, some politicians
pass on to their constituents all the facts they learn in order to
escape the responsibility for these hard choices. In the name of
national security other politicians have gone the other way by

withholding facts which could do the citizens no harm but which
would reveal the politicians' own mistakes.

Another problem, in Gibbon's words, is "the deep and dangerous question, how far the public faith should be observed, when
it becomes incompatible with the public safety." When may a
treaty be broken or a defense contract canceled? When may persons who have not been proved insane or charged with any crime
be confined on the apparent probability that they will do harm?

▼

How to present an issue to the public is a puzzle. Almost all
political problems are complicated. A simple problem soon is
solved or disappears as such. To oversimplify is to mislead, yet a
politician has to simplify, not because the average voter cannot
understand a clear and thorough explanation, but because he will
not listen long enough. It is difficult to explain an issue in terms
which are accurate, simple, and brief. Those politicians who produced the Federalist Papers and the Gettysburg Address grasped
the problem's root, understood their audience's minds, and expressed themselves with clarity and art. Men on that level have
passed through the smoky tunnel of polysyllabic gobbledygook
and come out in the pure air on the far side. But except for those
lofty few, a politician is left with the dilemma: to speak at length
and not be heard, or to speak briefly and either mislead or be
misunderstood.

▼

A speaker is tempted to make promises when he is unable to
hold his audience by entertaining it as a Barkley or a Stevenson
can do. For example, a local candidate for prosecutor promised
to throw all sex offenders in jail, "even the innocent ones."

Ambition to achieve may be a productive force. Ambition for
power and glory is often destructive and tends to make a man good
for little. Yet to achieve much in politics requires one to climb
to dizzy heights. So to do good one must tread the brink of hell.

Men forget that high office is a tool and not a prize. To measure achievements in politics is difficult because they are obscured by the power and eminence which often accompany, but do not prove, achievements, and because each problem always seems to be replaced by the next instead of solved.

▼

A politician may be tempted to be vulgar. If he is a sucker for pomp, he may think vulgarity a way to resist the temptation; or if he has succumbed he may try to conceal his condition by a coarse mask. Like Congressman Boykin with his repeated motto, "Everything is made for Love," he may think vulgarity a shield against the hostility of those constituents who equate refinement with that extinct snobbish ruling class whose manners and education were an ornament. He may agree with those people. Vulgarity is often ineffective, but its wide acceptance lowers the aesthetic tone of public life. A few men only pretend to be vulgar and make the most of both sides of the street, like Governor Cross of Connecticut with his cultivated diatribe against baths. Some confuse vulgarity with the politically priceless common touch. When they aim at the latter they hit the former. Some, like Lincoln, embody both. Others have the common touch uncheapened, like Franklin Roosevelt or the Emperor Augustus, who did not need a prompter when he called each Senator by name and who was liked and trusted by the people because he knew the names and numbers of the gladiators at the games.

▼

What company should a politician keep? Unless he spends time with those who suffer from injustice or misfortune of a kind which public policy can relieve or correct, he is likely to lack the sympathy necessary to do right by them. This rule applies to him for every separate group in society which has its own special problems. As to those groups of which he sees little, he is an absentee politician and tends to neglect or mishandle their concerns. Unless he has continued contact with a group, he cannot do a proper job for it. He lacks the knowledge needed for sound judgment and the indignation or pity to inspire him to act with force. Without association face to face, the inspiration still may be provided by one of two rare types—a man with a sensitive imagination or a self-propelled lover of mankind. But in most cases only personal contact can give one understanding of each singular group. If a politician acts in ignorance of his constituents, he will make policy in one of two ways. If he fits his policy to the only class or group which he knows, he harms all other groups which differ from it. If he conforms his policy to the whole constituency's common denominators, he does equal harm because its application is more complete though not as harsh. In either case, a policy which fails to provide specific variations to meet the differences of each particular group imposes rules of a more strict uniformity than is suitable for a society that allows diversity not only of individuals but of groups as well.

If he fails to consort with the wise and able, he may not develop his wisdom and abilities to their highest point. Without the regular company of his peers, his effort is likely to slacken and his perspective to blur. A man who reaches high estate may be like the priest who was appointed bishop. His friend told him that never again would he hear a candid word or eat an ill-cooked meal. When a man is among his peers, his jokes must be funny to get a laugh.

Because of these two conflicting needs, to improve his powers and to know the situation of those he represents, a politician is blessed if he has a receiving apparatus sensitive enough to detect the people's thoughts in a short time and if he has the gift of letting the people know that he respects and understands them despite the fact that he does not often come among them.

In office, a politician has one of the moral problems of a ruling class, close association with other community leaders, which makes him reluctant to treat them with justice when punishment is called for. He weakens his impartiality by confining himself to association with fellow big shots. He does not tolerate their sins but he feels inhibited by fellowship. To give his government its due, he need not go far toward the classic example of stern adherence to the state in preference to personal ties: When the first Roman consul, Junius Brutus, learned that his sons had conspired to restore the tyranny of Tarquin kings, he told the lictors to do their duty with an ax. (The royal family had put to death his father and elder brother, so perhaps family loyalty dictated his choice and he was not a model patriot after all.) Another instance: In a scarcity economy Lycurgus ceased to eat in order to achieve his death by means of service to the state.

A politician feels a strong pull to treat with scrupulous consideration those people with whom he deals in person and is on good terms, and to overlook the rest. At worst this narrow loyalty becomes honor among thieves; at best it earns the compliment that, "If he's bought he stays bought." At seventy-six, John Quincy Adams wrote: "Throughout the course of a long and diversified public life I have considered it among the most impressive of my duties to render liberal justice to every individual with whom I have ever been associated in the public service, whatever my personal relations with him may have been, public or private." Even for Adams, cold to men and hot for principle, the ideal of justice for all was hard to attain.

A politician's intentions may be good, and he may give to the corrupt only the appearance of corruptibility, but if he acts in a way to suggest the thought, or encourage the hope, that those who cultivate him can have their way with him he makes himself bait for the wrong appetites. His plight resembles that of Red Cross girls on duty at a jungle island wartime base because the congestion of petitioners tends to keep all but the most ruthless and aggressive from reaching his presence. Attracting unattractive attention from unattractive persons tends to make him either a dogmatic misanthrope or a pushover, to turn him too far away from people and too close to principle, or to corrupt him.

It is more difficult for a politician to be severely just with those he knows and understands than tolerantly merciful to those whom he does not. Until recent years there was a greater willingness to pass judgment on both issues and men. Despite the ardor of personal relationships, there was less of an effort to understand people. Persons were measured more by their conduct alone, without adjustment for their nature and condition. This new concern for explanation of conduct is accompanied by a more flexible standard of responsibility, an increased tolerance of misconduct. Although his duty says he must, a politician finds it hard at once to judge and understand. Most politicians are disposed to lean toward judging issues and understanding men.

▼

A politician has to stay close enough to an organization, whether party or personal, to employ its force and depend on its support, yet far enough apart from it to show his independence and keep from being identified with its excesses. Truman went to one extreme, and Eisenhower the other.

▼

A politician must serve several masters, and serve them well. He tries to reconcile the never-ending conflicts between the things he is supposed to do, the elements of which cannot be codified: the duty to obey the wishes of his constituents and to follow his conscience or judgment or both; the duty to do the right thing, and the necessity to stay in office to get the right things done. He must get along with constituents who think all economies should be made at the expense of Somewhere Else, and also with the elected representatives of Somewhere Else whose constituents feel the same way. He has to choose between a direct and immediate benefit to his district and a long-run, indirect one through the welfare of a wider unit, the state or nation. In appropriations and appointments there often is a conflict between the general good and his loyalty to friends and colleagues. There may be the choice between success and fame (for a Governor or Senator) or the choice between fame and greatness (for a Presidential nominee), and the fear of missing both. How can a politician give direction, yet be the public's agent; how can he both lead and obey his principals, how embody his constituents' aspirations without becoming their lowest common denominator? Related to this policy dilemma is a personal one: how to carry out the public's will without abdicating responsibility until he brings about a paternalistic government under which a public servant becomes a public ward.

Self-deception makes these contradictions harder to resolve. Politicians can fool themselves all of the time. With fervent earnestness, dairy area legislators contend that oleomargarine is unhealthy, un-American, and against the laws of supply and demand. A feeble invalid (Glass, Wagner, Vandenberg) convinces himself that he can serve the public interest better by keeping his seat (although unable to rise from it unaided), than by resigning to permit his replacement. Probably few managers of affairs in the Soviet Union realize the absurdity of the ideological terms which they recite. A politician is tempted to tell himself that his ambition or fear of failure is obedience to the public will, so that he pretends the people are the sun whose beams it is his duty to reflect as a sort of governmental moon. Those distributors of popular entertainment who refuse to take responsibility for taste assert the same defense. In either case the opinions of mankind are given abject homage instead of a decent respect.

When does a politician have the right or duty to substitute not only his judgment but also his morals for those of his constituents by discarding expediency in favor of a course which he considers morally right toward other districts, states, or countries? Directed only by his pity, should a politician donate public funds to starving foreigners abroad in a case where this will not gain advantage for his country, and a majority of his constituents have not shown such a course to be their wish?

The dilemma between a politician's judgment of what is right and his constituents' wishes tends to be more easy to resolve in favor of the former to the extent that his constituency is diversified. A group demanding one thing will have no special rights to it from the politician who represents its members if another equally deserving group asks for the opposite. In such a case to disregard the wishes of some of his constituents is not a breach of trust because it is a necessity, and obedience to the will of all his constituents is not a duty because it is impossible. This is a great asset of the Presidency, which is subject to less pressure to be parochial than any other elective office.

"We both alike know that into the discussion of human affairs the question of justice arises only where the pressure of necessity is equal, that the strong take what they can and the weak grant what they must." *Thucydides*

▼

A member of Congress has the ethical and practical problem of balancing several duties which often conflict in purpose and always in allotment of time. An important one is to help and represent his constituents with their personal problems with Uncle Sam, that is, to serve as mediating agent between citizens and government. The administrative branch has become huge, impersonal, and complicated. Sometimes a citizen's legitimate efforts are frustrated by the inertia or indifference of a government office. Often his Congressman is the only person to whom he can turn, who can intercede as a sort of tribune to expedite the matter or in some other way to correct an impending injustice. Another duty of a Congressman is to see to it that his district is not deprived of its fair share of federal funds.

These two functions, errands for constituents and money for the district, both are subordinate to the process of shaping national policy. Many members of Congress and their constituents forget that times have changed and think that what is good for their district is good for the country, or do not care whether it is or not. They think, or assume without thinking, that exclusive attention to the district at the expense of the region or nation will improve the fortune of the district in the long run, that the primary aim is to win a multilateral tug of war for pork barrel funds with 434 other Congressmen who still feel themselves Kentuckians or Virginians first and Americans second. The truth of the trickle-down theory as applied to the central government and those who inhabit each of the areas which it governs is not yet widely understood.

▼

A tactical problem is how can a politician show the world all the rectitude he has, and maybe more to boot, without offending the gentlemen of easy virtue with whom he sometimes has to deal. A person does not deserve, and cannot long enjoy, the title of politician unless he conceals any feelings of disgust with knaves or impatience with fools. In this his work differs from some occupations in which one is shielded from both.

Among the questions whose chief element is moral the most basic one which confronts a politician is how to have courage to be honest in the broadest sense, yet stay in office.

Another problem is: When should a politician call on his fellow men to exercise *their* courage? This has become one of government's most delicate problems. Some claim peace to be our paramount aim of policy. It is not so. Anyone can have peace by knuckling under. Freedom is, and must be, our proper goal. Always men have had to risk their lives to win or save the freedom of their community. This has been the only aim which justifies the use of military force. In More's *Utopia*, the people waged war for three purposes: to defend their own territory when invaded, to deliver the territory of an ally from invaders, and to free an oppressed nation from tyranny.

Now the new weapons raise a dilemma. If we refuse to fight we may have to submit to others, yet if we give up peace to preserve freedom, we may lose both by destroying established society, if not mankind as well. This is unlike some dilemmas which can be indirectly solved by waiting until they disappear or by adopting one or a portion of several presently competing policies. Here we cannot hope to muddle through by a continuous balancing act —preparing to win a war, avoiding the last step into it, and yet being evidently willing to take the last step so that others will not call our bluff—because the tightrope is too long and our own due care alone is not enough. Safety is not assured by the consoling fact that this dilemma faces everyone, nor by the balance of terror which makes bullet-headed generals of powers hostile to us hesitate to do more than thunder at each other, "Delenda est Chicago." Our strongest potential enemies are unwilling to be Samson pushing at the pillars, and no one wants chaos, even though some do not care about freedom and some are indifferent to death. But although no strong group on earth is led by beasts who wish mankind had but a single neck, the whole structure of opposing forces is so unstable that some neutral chance incident may set in motion events which will bring on doomsday. To solve this problem will take more than courage and a steady nerve because no answer lies in policies which have yet been tried.

Part

Methods

5

THE CAMPAIGN

The continuing process of change in campaign methods has speeded up in recent years. Campaign efforts get less mileage than they did, and less than they will when the rate of change declines, permitting their comparative effectiveness to be better known.

A party apparatus counts for less. The last machine has gone. What remains is only accusation in the mouths of ardent partisans who charge others with possessing one. A campaign staff is the most important instrument because, besides the actions of the candidate, campaigns are now conducted largely by means of professional specialists who fabricate speeches, pamphlets, film strips, and news releases. Money raising and advice on strategy are the only important functions which remain in amateurs' hands.

With mass media which use a common language that everyone can read, people no longer need party workers to advise them how to vote. When a citizen can see and hear the candidate on a screen at home, and read news, written by the best journalists from a variety of points of view, about the candidate's public and private life, he does not heed what is told him by the precinct captain on his block. The media have done to the campaign system what the invention of gunpowder did to the feudal kingdom—destroyed the barons and shifted their power to the masses and the prince. A candidate now pays less attention to district leaders than to opinion polls.

The party organization used to have the two purposes of persuading people to prefer one party label over another, and then of leading people to the polls or inducing them to go. Now the candidates or the media's agents do the persuasion through the media. People are induced to vote by many factors. A party organization is in most places a relatively minor one, sharing its influence with the leadership of other organized groups of which the voter is a member, such as labor unions and P.T.A.'s, and with unorganized groups to which most voters belong.

Parties are still organized on a geographic basis, which no longer conforms to the operation of American society. Improved communication and transportation allow each person to select his companions from a wider circle around his home. Except for farmers, a small minority, we no longer associate with each other primarily within our neighborhood.

The party animal has lost not only its strength but also the carrot and stick which induce it to work. Civil service has made campaign activity unnecessary to keep a job and unavailing to get one. For those who work for Uncle Sam, the Hatch Act has converted campaign work from insurance to a risk. Inflation, by widening the pay-rate lag of public work; and full employment, by diminishing the relative insecurity of private work—together have reduced public jobs' appeal. Accurate audits and efficient law enforcement have stopped the payment of campaign workers from public funds.

As party activity has become less important the number of party workers has declined. Among those whose primary interest is in jobs, the lag of public wages behind private ones has caused only near unemployables to remain. Some of the party workers are old people who enjoy the activity primarily for its social aspects and treat the organization as a club. Especially in campaigns, some college students take part for a while as an experiment or adventure. The largest and most effective new group is the women whose family responsibilities allow them free time and who wish to do civic service. Among all ages, prosperity enables participation by more persons in whom idealism is a major motive, but the proportion of these is still small.

In most places the party organization is an important pressure group with more of a power to veto than to select. Although it is difficult for a governor or partisan mayor to disregard his party organization, some members of the Senate have almost nothing to do with it, yet do not seem to suffer for their independence. Many organization men and women resent this attitude but realize they cannot replace such a man for renomination, and in a general election they grudgingly give him support.

Formerly, an organization had the sole selection of nominees and often was conclusive in deciding the election. Now people are given a genuine choice, although not always a good one. Many of the best men and women do not run. Some of the values of many of the voters can be disputed. But the voters now tend to choose and elect candidates of their personal preference, independent of an organization's influence. The reasons why politics in the last thirty years has attracted to Democratic tickets more candidates of a quality to win public preference than it has to Republican tickets, despite the higher average levels of ability, intelligence, and education, (though not imagination) among Republican than Democratic voters, are beyond the scope of this book.

▼

The common statement that campaigns have become far more expensive is misleading. In relation to the size of the national economy and the cost per vote, campaigns do not cost much more than they did twenty or one hundred years ago. The difference is that the work used to be done by an organization, and in the main the cost was borne by an indirect and unofficial public subsidy, supplemented by a few men, often Senators. A campaign was conducted by a band of workers impelled by hopes and fears that jobs would be won, kept, or lost. The candidate gave only his spare time.

Today, the mass media have become the chief means by which he can influence the reason or passions of the electorate. The media are economically efficient in their function, but their use is expensive because so many more votes are at stake. In 1956, Eisenhower was given more votes in New York and Ohio alone than Wilson received from the nation in 1912, and the man elected Governor of Ohio in 1956 received more votes than Lincoln did from the nation in 1860. In losing a race for Congress I received 10,000 more votes than John Quincy Adams did when he was elected President.

The burden of a campaign's cost, which used to rest on the taxpayer and a few rich men, has shifted to the candidate himself, who must pay from his own resources and what he can collect from others. He is either pressed or compelled to get his help from persons and groups to whom he should wish not to be beholden. Like a man in business for himself, a politician sometimes feels as though his life were a continual process of incurring obligations and repaying them, but the oppressive difference from business is that these obligations are on the fringes of his work instead of at its core.

Few contribute much from friendship or public spirit. Small sums come from patriots, partisans, or persons who enjoy being identified with a celebrity, like an alumnus who keeps an athlete. A one-sided majority of the dollar volume, although given often by a minority of the contributors, comes from those who wish preferential treatment—or insurance against adverse treatment—by government in rates, rules, contracts, licenses, or loans. These larger "gifts" impose an obligation to do those requested favors which, by definition, are against the public interest because, without any contribution, the contributors might expect to get what they deserve, so far as democratic government is just.

A limited allowance of income tax deduction would reduce the proportion of large gifts by raising the volume of small ones. Public disclosure of contributions and those who make them would tend to shift their nature from implied contracts to true gifts of the kind made by Justice Holmes when he named the United States the residuary beneficiary under his will. The drop in prospects of material gain, caused by general knowledge of this information, would diminish the flow of money from big contributors. A public subsidy to the nominees in the general election and to those who score a near miss in the primary would be the strongest element of all in weakening big contributors' power to induce partiality toward themselves.

Legislation limiting campaign spending on those methods which are directed at the irrational faculties can cut the total campaign cost, relieving taxpayers of expense and candidates of pressure. The services for which the agencies of publicity are paid are directed mainly at fears and appetites. A curb on scare ads, catchwords, and name familiarity ads (the purpose of which is to implant the memory of a name and to do so without offensive associated meanings) would expose the voters to more clear light, fewer refracted images, and less heat.

Sometimes a person is elected without spending. However, his success is not due to some clever trick of campaigning without using money, but rather to the fact that to win he did not need to run. It was enough to stand. A campaign is a means to win only where the net result of all other factors will put within a narrow range opponents' totals of prospective votes.

▼

Another important change in campaign methods has taken place in the operation of national conventions. Compared to the past, national conventions have become tame and polite. The public address system makes shouting unnecessary, and without a mike the size of the crowd makes it futile. Conventions used to be stag. Now the presence of women improves the manners of the men. Air conditioning, permitting more formal dress which tends to cause more formal conduct, makes a convention so much easier on nerves and tempers that it might be impossible now to nominate a candidate under the former two-thirds rule because the delegates would not become so desperate to go home that most of them would be willing to agree. Television encourages mild exhibitionism but inhibits most of the vulgar deviations of behavior. In the convention hall, fist fights and drunkenness have almost disappeared. Delegates are circumspect for fear they may be seen back home. During invocations men even stop smoking cigars.

The strongest cause of better manners at conventions is the higher quality of delegates. Civil Service and the Hatch Act have withdrawn most of those with primarily venal motives from the group available or willing to go. Because so many more people now can afford to make the trip, delegates are elected from a larger, more competitive field. Also, this prosperity permits a state convention to split its national delegates' votes in half in order to double its delegation's size and thus enable more to go.

On the other hand, selection as a delegate is commonly a reward for faithful labor in the party vineyards. This system tends to result in delegates who neither represent the best of their party's sentiment in their communities nor respond to the community's wishes, although by trying to pick a winner they seek to meet the apparent national choice. Some political institutions are becoming overly responsive, but conventions are whimsical and sluggish, neither exercising an independent will nor reflecting the home folks' taste.

Although not every delegate may listen only to his public spirit, delegates are now more free from boss control. During the Democratic conventions of 1932 and 1956 I watched Jim Farley and Carmine DeSapio, respectively, manage the campaign of the current Governor of New York. Conditions of the time allowed Farley to act as a general and required DeSapio to act as a salesman.

Conventions have become so big that the crowd is docile because with unruly behavior the process would not work. It is easier to preside over a national convention than over a state or county convention. A delegate seeking recognition cannot even be heard unless the chairman tunes him in.

No one forgets that his family, friends, and enemies may be watching through the eyes of the TV cameras, which are pointed down on the crowd like machine guns around the walls of a prison yard. Awareness of this inspection checks the spontaneity of the proceedings. It encourages the wish to show off but represses other impulses. It cuts the time taken up in bickering and debate and produces designs to contrive dramatic effect. The focus of the gathering tends to be shifted from within to without. Television has increased the emphasis on entertainment at conventions; it is speeding the trends in politics to separate the producing functions of work and entertainment, to hire outsiders for the latter, and to increase the consumption of entertainment with political work.

Even a peaceful convention is exciting. This is inevitable where a multitude of strangers from diverse backgrounds are thrown together, where a substantial proportion are energetic, intelligent, articulate, and interested in ideas, and only a few have a mainly frivolous intent; where, despite their disagreement, their thinking is not too far apart to justify conversation and argument; where they are stirred by animosities within their delegations, among people who know each other and resent the enforced company. An open convention has the tension of a sporting event. One's own propaganda is intoxicating even when only half believed. For about a week, several thousand people churn together in a few downtown hotels. Once every four years this process, partly mechanical, partly chemical, temporarily makes a national party out of a loosely connected assortment of state and local groups.

The fault of the Presidential nominating process is the method of selecting delegates, not the national convention system itself, which is true representative government. It provides the discussion, debate, and personal knowledge which are essential to the pursuit of truth. (These are practiced and acquired, respectively, not on the convention floor but elsewhere before and during the convention.) It is the best device for selecting nominees for national office in a country as big as ours. The direct primary system is better only in smaller political units where the candidates can know and be known by the electorate and can take part in the campaign dialogue. Still, a national convention's atmosphere is given by the closing lines of *Dover Beach:*

"And we are here as on a darkling plain
Swept by confused alarms of struggle and flight,
Where ignorant armies clash by night."

▼

Forgetting that they themselves compose the jury, people sometimes regard their favorite candidate as their champion engaged in a trial by combat to vindicate their principles and interests. To describe a campaign as a "race" or "fight" is inaccurate because the efforts of a competitor seldom are decisive. A politician, unlike a general or an athlete, never can be invincible, except within a constituency which constitutes a sinecure. Furthermore, a candidate cannot even be sure that his campaigning will change the election result, while a lawyer in a lawsuit knows at least that a diligent pursuit of proven methods of preparation and trial will raise the odds of success, even if the outcome hinges on the image of some half-forgotten experience in the mind of a judge.

Scientists refuse to accept an hypothesis until they have verified it by exhaustive examination of all available evidence which may prove or disprove it, and they continue to discard each successive hypothesis as it fails to meet their tests. By contrast, a politician must act on his hypotheses, which are tested only by looking backward on his acts. A candidate cannot even experiment. Because no one knows what works in a campaign, money is spent beyond the point of diminishing returns. To meet similar efforts of the opposition all advertising and propaganda devices are used—billboards, radio, TV, sound trucks, newspaper ads, letter writing or telephone committee programs, handbills, bus cards. No one dares to omit any approach. Every cartridge must be fired because among the multitude of blanks one may be a bullet.

Some urge an attitude of Olympian reserve, a few sonorous

pronouncements of fundamental principle. Some claim a catalogue of documented facts is just the thing to woo the inscrutable voter. Others insist the only way is to put a hammer lock on the opponent and roll around in the sawdust. Many think a speech ought to be what Napoleon said a constitution should be, short and obscure. A member of the State Senate for many years, who has never lost an election, told me how he campaigns in his district door to door: "You tell your host or hostess who you are and declare in forthright tones, 'I'm here to talk with you about our State government; you may not agree with me but at least you will know where I stand.' Then you sit down in the living room, listen to him or her, and agree!" When a fellow named Gillespie Craighead ran for Congress in Seattle he asserted he was the only man in the race who could prove he was sane; then he would display his certificate of discharge from a mental hospital. He received several thousand votes, but a former U. S. Senator beat him.

A common mistake of post-mortems is to assert that a certain event or a stand or mannerism of a candidate caused him to win or lose. Often no one knows whether its effect was plus, minus, or zero, whether the election result was because of this factor or despite it. Spectacular events, whether a dramatic proposal, an attack, or something in the news outside the campaign, are like a revolving door. They win some voters and lose others. A disclosure that a candidate's brother committed suicide in a mental hospital will cause some voters to doubt the candidate's own mental strength and health, while others will be drawn to him by sympathy and repelled by his opponent's cruelty. Another example is the matter of Grover Cleveland's bastard in the 1884 campaign. The net balance in these cases remains unknown in both direction and amount, and even if correctly estimated, such a factor still could not be called the sole cause of the result. It was merely one of many causes of which the election is the algebraic sum. Where the margin was close, this factor could be called the cause only to the extent that the result would not have happened but for it, like the horseshoe nail that caused the kingdom's loss.

Each voter makes up his mind by the delicate resolution of several factors, some unconscious and all variable. No test has been devised for campaign methods or strategy, and little can be done to determine the effects of other factors. To know the effect of each thing he is doing and saying is a candidate's dearest wish. If he knew where pay dirt was he could concentrate there instead of digging all over the countryside. But he proceeds in ignorance. Not even his friends can be relied on to tell him all they know, which is less than is revealed by the scientific opinion polls, themselves inadequate as political weather vanes. A man will freely tell which fender styling he prefers. Often enough to be statistically useful, he will say for whom he plans to vote, and then keep his word. But he will not or cannot tell why. In testing the effects of campaign methods there are too many deviating, indeterminable factors. The interviewed voter may not have been affected by any speech or slogan, yet may feel that unless he says he was, he will be thought an ignoramus. He may have been affected by a certain campaign act but when asked about it he may forget either the act or the effect or both. He may or may not still be affected by it in his decision on election day, and he may not vote. The effect of what one side does may be canceled out in his final decision by what the other side does later. He may not be able to sift the campaign acts which repel him or attract him. Seldom when a man speaks to a stranger about some deep and subtle thought within him is he articulate enough to say what he means or candid enough to mean what he says. He may try to tell the interrogator what he thinks the other would like to hear, or he may refuse to talk at all. A candidate does not know whether he is throwing balls or strikes.

By their impact just before an election, poll figures tend to bring to pass their own predictions. When the polls become more accurate about opinion, as distinguished from voting intention, where the margin of error is already small, not only will they directly affect the results, they also will alter campaign methods. Candidates will watch the reports and try to reflect them exactly.

If response to the public wishes expressed in the reports was the only action taken, candidates would be left even with each other. So candidates will try to think up an appealing novelty, guess the errors in the polls, or guess how opinion will change between the sampling and the election, and will try to be the first in harmony with it. This will be like playing the stock market in trying to anticipate the trend or to outguess the experts, although the game is even more elusive because it is based altogether on slippery elements of opinion, while in the market the starting point, at least, rests on solid measurement of economic fact. A market speculator first will guess the future effects of economic forces, then what other speculators think about these forces, then what may be the expectations of other speculators about each other. Keynes wrote that some imaginative minds carry this process to the fifth or sixth degree. By contrast, a candidate's duo-poly relationship with his opponent seems to call for simpler calculations, especially since he can predict the other's actions more accurately than he can the thoughts of an unknown voter. Before long the polls and other studies may be able to tell him current attitudes above or below the surface of many voters' minds. But they may avail him little because voters are becoming more like speculators in basing their opinions on the attitudes of others, who do the same. Instead of splashing around in this quicksilver he may resort to asserting his own ideas again.

▼

Voters do not know as much as they need to know in order to make wise decisions in the matters which they are called on to decide. They have enough general knowledge of politicians and enough details of information about issues but not enough of the converse of either. A way to win a voter's favor is to press his flesh, and a candidate may gain by knowing many people, but because of change in the campaign process few people know any candidate well. There are many offices for each voter to consider and many constituents for each candidate to reach. Also, foreign affairs, now of dominating importance and an element of all national issues, make it difficult for many citizens to avoid deception by the communications media because they have slight experience against which to measure what they hear and read. Of course, to the extent that the media are truthful, citizens are better informed than before because the news is more thoroughly covered and widely distributed. Since the mass media now give people about as much information as they will take, it behooves a candidate to inform less and interpret more. The information he needs to supply is what has been omitted by the media which reach his audience.

There is more concern about politics than there was earlier in this century and better means of getting information about public affairs. Although people are less agitated by feelings of public insecurity and injustice, and although many are dismayed by the size and remoteness of government, they nevertheless have more time to give to politics and realize that government has become more important to their continued happiness. But the irrationality and confusion of the campaign process alienate the politicians from the people. The three main defects of this process are its expense to candidates, deception of the voters by platitudes and slander, and failure to reveal the nature and capacity of candidates. Issues are not joined. The problem is to renew and improve the connection between the citizen and the facts about issues and candidates. It is also to find means by which the rational faculties of citizens can be reached and exercised on public affairs.

One way to clarify the intercourse between citizen and politician is to have candidates answer questions propounded without notice by informed and disinterested interrogators. Such a series of examinations may be taken over TV and radio and reported in the papers. In pairs, opponents would submit to the same questions. There is no better means for a voter to compare candidates and test their knowledge and candor than to watch them give unrehearsed answers to questions which they tackle together. In straight debate, a man with more experience or aptitude may have an unfair advantage, and one or both debaters may so cloud the air with impassioned double talk that the audience is left in frustrated ignorance. The presence in voters' minds of a rational basis of fact for making their choices reduces the appeal of slogans and softens the impact of incitements to suspicion, doubt, and hate.

A minor device to give more understanding of issues and wider participation in making policy is through the medium of state and county party conventions at which there is an opportunity for a large proportion of the delegates to take part in consideration of a platform. At these smaller conventions, run by anarchy or despotism, items of business either wallow in confusion or click off according to a script. The main value of a platform is the education received by people who make it; but this chance rarely is afforded because so little time is allocated to it. Speeches are many and long. Prompted by slips of paper sent up to him, the chairman introduces many worthies in the crowd, and each feels impelled to say some words of greeting. The keynote speaker often thunders on until he squeezes the platform against the closing time. Soon after debate gets under way on fish vs. dams or highways vs. schools, the chairman interrupts to say he must entertain a motion to adjourn because this hall has been rented by Cab Calloway for use since half an hour ago. To justify cutting short the platform debate, preliminary greetings and battle cries have to be more inspiring or illuminating than they usually are.

▼

The time when a politician should be most responsive is during a campaign and the period of warming up to it. Unpopular stands are better made long before, and soon after, a campaign. A short period limits the chances for circumstances to prove the soundness of an unpopular action, and a candidate's courage will receive little acclaim unless and until his decision has become popular because generally regarded as having been right. If you are going to oppose the wishes of the people whom you represent you had better not go before them for endorsement until either they have had a chance to forget the apparent injury or circumstances have been allowed to show that you never injured them after all.

The tumult and passion of adversary proceedings make a campaign an unsatisfactory occasion to win acceptance of a new idea, although it will do to introduce one. It is hard to get original proposals accepted any time. And in campaigns the natural resistance to a new idea, rational disagreement based on its defects, and opposition hostility and ridicule unrelated to its worth, combine to place a burden of proof too heavy for an advocate to overcome. Idealists or those who favor affirmative thought are often disappointed with candidates who do not go beyond a few of the genuine issues of the day except to engage in personal criticism or argue issues which would be dead if only both sides would drop them. In fact, a candidate who proposes something new is often irresponsible or visionary. If he proposes an original, creative plan, no matter how sound, he is likely a dreamer to think he will get anywhere with it in the campaign. If he makes out that he has invented some inexpensive marvel which will bring joy to all, he is either a fool or a fake.

Because a campaign makes impossible a dip beneath the surface, not only the advance of a new idea but teaching of any kind is more effective between campaigns. To paraphrase Mark Antony when he knocked on Cleopatra's door, a candidate says, "I didn't come to teach." In a campaign, people are not interested in theory. The lessons are more often moral than intellectual. People want to know *what* a candidate proposes to do about pending specific problems. In quiet times, one can descend to fundamentals and tell *why*. People then will listen longer to a reasoned explanation and apply a smaller discount to the speaker's words as colored in a way to serve himself. But despite the fact that the teaching process is less efficient during a campaign than at other times, the value of education and the large size of the audience justify making education the main function of a campaign, provided this emphasis will not result in losing the election, that is, provided one is either way behind or way ahead.

A common cause of such a noncompetitive situation, which would justify the use of a campaign for educational purposes, is a legislature's boundary revision, creating a series of Alabamas and Vermonts, thus giving contentment to incumbents by relieving them of job insecurity and to the party organizations by assuring each of winning some prizes every time; but such an arrangement stagnates politics by suppressing competition and it curtails the citizens' choice.

On occasions when there is no real contest except in measure of disagreement, if a candidate is an odds-on choice to win, he can transmit his ideas effectively. Little opposition interrupts him; he receives the respectful attention of those who know he is going to be an office holder and thus important, and of those who admire winners; the greatest advantage is that he can obtain sufficient contributions to satisfy quite avaricious dreams. If he is thought to be a sure loser he can reach the voters only with his own time and money, for he will receive little help from his party and nothing from private groups or persons. Even if he is thought to be both noble and eloquent, those of the idealists who have money to give prefer to help a candidate of equal merit who has a chance to win. Lovers of lost causes will not help him because they are content already to see him headed for defeat.

Among those who run for office, it is widely thought that little good can be done one's fellow men unless one wins. What General MacArthur said, "There is no substitute for victory," is only half true. Some candidates aim at both halves. So far as he is heard, seen, and understood, a candidate is a moral and intellectual teacher for better or worse. Like most means, a campaign is also in itself an end. It gives a chance to demonstrate virtue, to declare, defend, and illuminate the truth, and to do the statesman's duty to guide, to elevate and to instruct.

▼

6

THE CANDIDATE

When a man runs for office he anticipates two discoveries with nervous excitement. He begins to find out who his friends are, and many of them turn out to be people whom he did not know; and on election night he learns how much he has appealed to the enigmatic voter.

The decision as to when to run for office or when to run for a higher office than one has, is taken partly in the manner of a surf rider, who bides his time until the right wave looms up, then rides his board upon it to the beach. There are two differences between a race for office and a ride on the surf. In a campaign, a propitious wave is only one of several elements of success. And unlike a swimmer on the reef at Waikiki, a person who intends to run at an undetermined time is not certain that a reasonable wait will provide him with a chance for a ride which he can recognize before it has gone by.

While we were sitting in the doorway of a westbound boxcar, going through Montana one spring night, a fellow traveler told me how he could have wed a girl worth half a million but delayed too long and had to marry her poor aunt instead. Sometimes a man will plunge because his nerve or patience fails for fear his place upon the turning wheel may not come round to him in time. Others, driven by appetite or sustained by conceit, neglect the factor of a seasonable moment.

A politician jumps across the party organization through the media to reach the voters, for whom the sensation of his personality has become an almost decisive factor. In the past a man had to impress the leaders who would cause his election. His assets might be skill in maneuver and intrigue, judgment, vision, or administrative competence, and various moral qualities. Those leaders, who knew him and appreciated his talents, would not much mind if he was distant or peculiar. Now a candidate's appearance has to please, reassure, and satisfy a host of strangers from far off.

Aside from party, class, race, and other group motives, most votes are cast, not on some specific issue connected with a candidate, but rather by selection from a gallery of candidates in the voter's mind. The mental pictures represent every school of art except the photographic. In the booth a voter sees in his thoughts the pairs of candidates for each office across the machine as though they were the animals passing two by two. A candidate's aim should be to use a set of simple strokes to create a favorable portrait of himself set against the surrounding shadows of the persons and issues with which he may be identified: an image in the voters' eyes which combines identity with the voter, through sympathy and common experience, and an element of superiority which does not stoop but beckons grandly from above, an air suggesting, "Adhere to me and let me and other angels put your name in lights, in Paradise."

In some places a certain past experience may be a bar to election or an essential condition to success. Depending on constituents' likes, a candidate's having been an Oxford scholar may be a help or something to be hidden. A senior diplomat from India remarked with scorn for the rabble which had recently entered his country's Parliament, "Why, some of them haven't even been to jail." Enough voters give enough weight to a war record to induce some politicians to exaggerate or even, as in the case of Senator McCarthy, fabricate, hardships and brave deeds in their country's uniform. This attitude in a voter is based on one or more of several factors. Tradition, running from the long period in history when the aristocracy stood at the forefront of the battles, connects public leadership with war service. Some people think of public office as a reward for war service, like a veterans' bonus. War service has always been regarded as proof of national loyalty; it was the custom in the Roman Republic that a candidate for consul would expose his wound scars to the citizens. War service is treated as reassuring evidence of simplicity and candor as opposed to bookishness and cunning. It makes it easier for a candidate to be depicted as "bluff" rather than "glib." In addressing his constituents, a war record makes it easier for a politician to affect the manner of Othello to the Venetian lords. War service is recognized by everyone as a benefit to all. Unlike some other forms of public service, it does not offend as many people as it pleases. Yet the nature of war has become such that war service as a factor in political choice soon will disappear from voters' minds and will be replaced by other considerations connected with a candidate, perhaps his scholastic record or his behavior in some "moral equivalent of war" which may be developed. A convenient marker for this turning point is the career of Marshal Zhukov.

For some offices a certain type of person tends to be expected and preferred. A rough and ready outdoor sort may win with ease for sheriff but get nowhere in a race for city council. A bloodless Yankee may lose when he tries for mayor, yet be elected county clerk.

▼

Except in one-party states, general elections for important offices tend to be statistically close. The majority often does not exceed the scientific opinion polls' margin of error, so that there is yet no certain way to foretell the result. Until the moment of truth, a candidate does not know whether he is the bullfighter or the bull.

The uncertainty of politics dismays a person used to systematic plans. The loss of spontaneity through thinking of the next thing is a defect of modern life. Everyone has to consider the morrow. No one can do as the lilies of the field. Foresight is compulsory because one falls by the wayside if he fails to use it as everyone else does. Yet in a campaign it is difficult to plan one's steps. One is denied both the carefree joy of spontaneity and the security and certainty of foresight. Politics is an art and it is played by ear, though politicians often wish that they could use with profit more scientific method in the conduct of their work.

As generals are said to prepare for the last war, so election campaigns are planned with excessive attention to undigested lessons of history. The thinking of a candidate's advisers resembles that of scholastic philosophers, long on speculation and short on verified facts. The members of a strategy committee tend to be boosters rather than detached critics, a command group instead of a staff. Sometimes a candidate feels like a steer being groomed for a 4-H Club contest. His council is more likely to give him encouragement than guidance. For example, once in the Bronx Coliseum a powerful Negro from Brooklyn was hitting me hard; I clutched him and looked over his shoulder at a spectator who pounded on the ring apron as he shouted, "Pretend he's a Harvard man!"

For candidates, campaigns are like a war. There are comradeship, sacrifice, warmth of loyalty given and received, and moments of glory, fulfillment, and fear. Absence from home strains domestic ties, and clan ties are strained by taking sides. It is dirty and expensive. When it is over, this alien experience drops quickly out of mind, despite the remaining scars and debt. The heat of battle intensifies a candidate's combative spirit. Exhaustion weakens his power to decide. The necessity to act in haste under conflicting pressures and on confusing information makes his decisions less the result of reflection or belief than of character, habit, and chance. Unless his friends restrain him he may throw away both his purse and his good name. His friends' advice colors his acts more than when he is not on such a headlong chase. The counselors of even the most bullheaded candidate do much to set a campaign's tone. The choice of levelheaded, honorable advisers improves his chances to finish the race without regret or shame.

The hardest campaign is the first. After that the path is familiar, and there is the momentum of supporters, friends, and a well-known name. Among candidates before a campaign starts there is an eager, apprehensive wait; hurry and busy strategic moves off stage. As in the early rounds in a poker hand, the response and strength of possible opponents and the presence of support are tested by experimental bluffs. Next to the wait from the closing of the polls until the returns begin, the highest suspense in a campaign is when a candidate declares himself. He climbs to the battlements and blows his trumpet, then peers out to see how many men at arms come running to rally round his flag.

He has to be alert to tricks which can be important even though in form they resemble a practical joke. When Ed Munro, a high-principled politician, ran for county office in a northwest state, an Indian who had the same surname filed against him in the primary. This tactic would split his vote enough to give the nomination to his other chief opponent (who presumably had induced this filing). Before the names had been put on the voting machines, the second Munro withdrew when told that such a deception was a felony, and therefore if he stayed in the race he would be the only candidate guaranteed to spend some time in the county courthouse. Ed's friends had found this man after a desperate hunt. He was hard to find because he had been sleeping in a tree.

At the start a candidate's efforts are concentrated within his party. As the scale and formality of the campaign increase, the target shifts to the general public. On these early occasions, before his audience is critical and large, a candidate's material is tested. There is a chance to sharpen gags, expand lines, and cut what falls dead. It is like opening in New Haven before New York.

At repeated party meetings, the candidate grinds out his stock recital to a crowd of the faithful who know him well. Most of them could prompt him if he faltered. Attendance gains him little except to invigorate their working spirit and to avoid provoking their hostility by the appearance of a snub. Senator Henry Jackson has adopted the sensible practice of saying good-by to his friends at the beginning of a campaign, after he has told them that he loves them but that he will be busy for a while in their common cause. Some candidates take the easy but ineffectual course of campaigning mainly within party groups. Like the salesmen who go to the golf course to cultivate their friends instead of making calls on strangers, these candidates either fool themselves or yield to the temptation to stay where the going is smooth.

Local public meetings held to enable the community to hear the candidates often waste the time of both audience and speaker. Each candidate is stalled for part of an evening waiting his turn to speak to a few people. He faces an audience numbed by the beating of incessant waves of oratory. A succession of brief individual interviews is more effective in enabling citizens to know something of his opinions and catch the flavor of his personality. Despite the wasted time, public meetings are justified in the case of candidates for some of the smaller offices because these meetings furnish almost the only means for voters to observe these candidates.

▼

On cold nights a man of lukewarm faith was wont to point to a framed prayer on the wall and say, "Lord, them's my sentiments," as he jumped under the covers. By this means a candidate can declare his platform when allowed only a few minutes to speak. He states his accord with what another politician stands for. He names the man whose platform is more like his own than that of any other person among those whose platforms the audience already knows. An even more common practice is for the candidate to try to identify himself with a victorious figure who sometimes blesses his party mates who are reaching for his coattails from lower on the ladder.

An important factor is personal contact, which inspires those who meet a candidate to recommend him to others. To use this multiplier principle, the rings spreading from where a stone fell in a pool, timing is of the essence. Contacts made in the days just before election have slight worth because time does not permit the multiplier to operate, and without the multiplier's effect the number of persons a candidate can meet even in a whole campaign is too small to matter in a large constituency. Early in a campaign, except for an incumbent who is news in himself, public interest has not developed enough intensity to make the multiplier go. The candidate is less a subject of interest and may be less well known. People have less desire to talk to others about having met him. In most cases, therefore, shaking hands with a multitude is most effective during the month before the week before election day.

A wide personal acquaintanceship acquired before the campaign is a help. "My sister-in-law is a friend of Wheelhorse, the fellow who's running for the legislature. She knew him even before he went into politics"—magic words.

Probably the most effective campaign acts are those performed between campaigns. The volleys and thunders of a campaign raise a voter's resistance and obscure his sight. A Chief Justice of the Alabama Supreme Court kept on his office wall pictures of George Washington and John Marshall and an autographed photograph and letter from Jim Farley, congratulating him on his election. It was the only congratulation he had received after the general election, an uneventful day in those parts, as all the handshakes and other letters had come when he was nominated.

▼

The functions of some offices fail to inspire ardor, either sacrificial or pugnacious. One who runs for governor or mayor often is surrounded by those whose assistance is given on condition of an implied reward. But a candidate for Congress has so little patronage in prospect that few self-seekers repel him by their presence or embarrass him by their aid. Many persons uninterested in favors from him warm and uplift him by faithful work on his behalf.

In campaigns people work as volunteers to obtain several satisfactions. Some are a step toward fulfillment of a wish expressed through a conviction; that is, an attempt to assert or defend a principle or advance or protect an interest. Other satisfactions are directly emotional. There is the common experience in an adventure and membership in a common effort. There is the purgative from close observance of dramatic conflict, operating on people who themselves are peaceable.

A further motive applies to young people. They do simple work such as handing out folders but they get to hang around the headquarters and consort with the candidate and some of his lieutenants. Their own views on policy may be heard and sometimes even listened to. They learn plans before their execution and feel themselves participants in matters more important than would be allowed them in the ordinary course of life. They are more flattered than older people to be allowed to fraternize with these men and women. They finish armed with anecdotes to entertain their peers.

▼

A campaign is a revolving circus which bewilders actors and spectators alike. Blocks of votes are cast against (or for) a candidate for contradictory reasons, sometimes both wrong. Candidates who succeed in their effort to please everyone may get some votes because they are thought to be for the common man and others for being against him. The same things may be thought of their more clumsy opponents with the opposite results. In one campaign I was attacked as both a Bourbon and a Red. As a member of the commission which had drafted the proposed County Charter which was to be on the ballot, I supported its adoption in unison with the solid, "good government" elements of the business community. I was called a reactionary, both for the stand itself and by reason of the syllogism, common in campaigns, that since things equal to the same thing are equal to each other, persons who take the same side must be alike. In a conversation overheard on the bus a man told another he was going to vote against the Charter because Bullitt helped write it, "so probably it's a left-wing document."

The ferocity and violence of a rough campaign generate passionate animosity in a candidate's heart and inspire deep gratitude to those who bear arms in his cause. The rationality of a campaign tends to vary inversely with its length. Candidates and parties may have much in common, but it is on the basis of the differences that the voters make their choice. The sides start close together. They are driven to magnify existing differences and to invent new ones. As they draw farther apart verbally they provoke each other to greater excess. The separation grows by geometric progression until each side approaches nonsense land.

In contrast to an average citizen, a candidate is too busy with detail to be aware of an election's historic import. He is too elated by enthusiastic treatment or too concerned with what to say to a hostile or indifferent audience to think of community or national destiny. In a speech he may say "the world (nation, state) is watching what we do here," without realizing that this may be the truth.

▼

A candidate may see that he is going to lose if he does not delude himself and the margin is wide enough to be discerned. His helpers can drop out and cut their losses, but, like a player far behind near the end of a game, he is obliged by an unwritten rule of sport to keep giving the old college try.

He must go out to meet people, yet reserve enough time to rest, relax, and think, so that he can give a fresh and lively performance before the mass media. Stevenson's fall campaign in 1956 suffered from the preceding grind of state primaries and soliciting delegates.

Like a prisoner, the candidate marks off the calendar squares until the day when he is to be executed or paroled. On election day he feels like the man who had to open one of two blank doors. Behind one is a maiden, behind the other a tiger. To the candidate's friends, however, the contrast in alternatives may not be sharp. Often they are uncertain what fate to wish for him, whether to win, or to be spared the pains and, to them, degradation of public life. Thinking of him as though his body were to be tested for service by the Army or as though his mind were to be examined at a sanity hearing in court, the friends are in doubt whether to support his hopes, his vows, his rights, or his welfare.

A politician is almost by definition a man who enjoys people. But near the close of a campaign he has been surfeited by them. He resents his enemies. He is exasperated by his friends' proprietary demands, irritated by the importunities of his acquaintances, and weary of his own persistent approaches to strangers. He has had enough of the human race. He does not become a misanthrope but longs to be a forest fire lookout. He would rather be rude than President. But after the election his enjoyment of people soon revives when he is rested and free from the compulsion to persuade, impress, or please. Although spent, some defeated candidates soon begin to think like a baseball fan—"Wait till next year."

For certain happy warriors, many of them celebrated, campaigns are not nights in a cement mixer but trips to the country. Like Antaeus when he touched the earth, these buoyant spirits, by contact with their fellow men, are strengthened and refreshed. On election eve they turn in with dark-encircled sparkling eyes.

▼

A winner may have some second thoughts. He is surrounded by well-wishers, many of whom already seek favors. He may not feel satisfied or elated but he is sure to feel relief. During the campaign he asserted his capacity to solve the problems facing the office he has won and, whether or not he volunteered any answers, he displayed confidence that he had them. Now he sees that some of these problems are insoluble, and others would baffle Aristotle. Yet the presumption which it took for him to run is enough to make him feel adequate to handle his job on the level expected of him. For a little while no personal problem is likely to dismay him.

A loser in a race for high office is on the whole better off than one beaten for a lesser one. He may feel more disappointment at having missed a bigger prize. Whatever he may turn to may seem petty and unfulfilling. But his prominence and known abilities almost assure him an opportunity to make a good living. He is cushioned by the presence of friends and comforted by sympathetic letters from supporters who remind him they are for him just the same.

A man beaten for lesser office is more likely to have a young family which his defeat gives him time to enjoy and serve. He may find work which is as challenging and exacting as what he lost or did not get. But having quit his job and borrowed to the limit, he may finish deep in debt, and he cannot expect postelection contributions. He looks for a modest income doing something. He is not asked to head a college, invited to become an officer or partner of a substantial firm, or appointed to a commission by the President. His gloom is deepened by the thought that his friends have deserted him. He does not realize that those who worked for him for friendship's sake, who have gone back to their private concerns, would have disappeared as fast if he had won. He is left in solitude. No one calls him except the bookkeeper for the printing firm to remind him of his balance due. There is nothing to sustain him to counteract the memory of opposition slurs. By the standards of success the opposition has been proved right.

A loser in politics can console himself by cursing fate more often than a failure in private life can. An election does not prove that the defeated candidate's grasp fell far short of his reach. But when a man has been rejected by the voters and also sees no recognition elsewhere, unless he is an egotist or more indifferent to worldly success than most men who run for office, he feels himself a flop. But as a winner's elation soon is cooled by the problems put before him, so a loser's depression is dispelled as he reflects that although he is pressed by his creditors, the man who beat him is called by his constituents in the middle of the night; he starts to enjoy his relative freedom from responsibility; and sometimes he plans to run again.

▼

7

SOME PERSONAL EXPERIENCE

Each election year there is a minor change in the ways by which candidate and voter best can come in touch. A campaigner tries experiments or suffers from a time lag. As two means to approach the voters in person while running for Congress in 1954, I attended "coffee hours" and accosted people one by one in public places. I met about 9,300 (count kept by numbered bundles of folders) in five weeks, or about 1 in 65 of the district's population. The following observations were set down at the end of that campaign. They are consistent with my experience in half a dozen others before and after it, in two of which I ran and in the rest of which I campaigned for other candidates.

Most of the time it is delightful to sit in a big chair and stuff yourself with cookies while polite guests treat you as a universal expert. In the homes of supporters who had invited their friends and neighbors I submitted to questions but gave no set speech. Because no more effective engine has ever been invented to probe the nature of a candidate than free interrogation at close quarters, these meetings are an advantage to guests as citizens. And they tend to be uneasy though stimulating periods for the candidate; in the course of an hour some cherished prejudices are likely to collide. The voter may go away shaking his head at the thought of this menace to the Republic whom he has just met, while he still tolerates the others in the race. One does not use these meetings solely as an exercise in civics. In turnover they do not approach waiting in front of a mill through the half hour before the eight o'clock whistle. But each contact is more intensive where candidate and voter meet in a home, introduced by a mutual acquaintance, and where, instead of one greeting the other, who passes on, they actually converse. From this transient intercourse under these favorable conditions, if you are or later become a big shot, the voter may refer to you thereafter as a friend of his.

For successive personal contacts which are more superficial but can be made at a faster rate, you stand each day in supermarket parking lots and outside factory gates, or walk up and down the sidewalks in suburban shopping districts and force yourself upon your fellow citizens hour by hour. I went up to each person and said: "My name is Stimson Bullitt. I'm a candidate for Congress and I'm glad to meet you." If a man, I held out my hand at his belt buckle and waited to see if he would raise his hand to let me take it. Then I gave him or her a folder. If there was enough time, depending on the rate and volume of foot traffic, I asked his name. If a difficult name, I asked him to spell it or tried myself to do so and asked him if my effort was correct. Each person had a wall of indifference or suspicion to be assailed. At worst, one first is thought to be a panhandler or pickpocket and at best, a salesman. Perhaps a politician comes somewhere in between.

One makes the strongest impact in front of an industrial plant at dawn. The men one meets are impressed to find anyone out there to greet them so early, especially a member of a group they consider lazy and aloof. Also, the encounter becomes a common experience for them, a subject of conversation during the day with others in the plant who were not met.

The suburban shopping areas are better than downtown sections. The tempo is not as fast, and there are few offensive strangers to make the others shy. People are less hurried and less averse to being accosted. An easy place to work is a commuters' train or ferry. The captive audience takes its case in security and comfort.

The most barren soil is the waterfront. Many are tourists, some are bums, and the rest recoil at your approach. A race track is another waste of time. A low proportion of the crowd votes regularly for any office except the Presidency. And like people on other intense group occasions, the spectators resent one who interrupts their close attention. Taverns are unprofitable. The bartender is the only person worth meeting. Sober customers think you are a drunk coming over to molest them. Drunks grab you and hold on. They make speeches. Some of them used to entertain themselves with heavy jokes about my name and guns. If you approach anyone as you come out of a bar, he flees.

The best situation for meeting people at random is a small group engaged in idle conversation. This may be on the sidewalk or in a restaurant booth or barbershop. The people are less afraid to be accosted by a stranger because they feel protected by each other. With friendly banter you can often generate a jolly mood, leaving you the subject of their conversation after you have gone.

There are a variety of handshakes—warm, cold, hearty, firm, flabby, moist. I discovered that my hand did not get tired or sore although my hands are small and not very strong. It was a surprise not to be squashed sometimes by some powerful bully. I was embarrassed to make a few jump with pain, presumably from sore hands.

The range of response was wide—hostile, indifferent, suspicious, friendly, enthusiastic, encouraging. Some were flattered to shake the hand of such an eminent person; others politely stated that they differed with me in politics. Sometimes a person would show several reactions, shifting from one to the other in a few moments of discourse.

Some turned away showing ill will because they recognized me as a person about whom they had read bad things in the papers. Some refused to touch me, then, when told I was a Democrat, reversed their attitude and shook hands with warmth. Everyone who asked, "Are you a Democrat or a Republican?" appeared to be a Democrat. It seemed that the Republicans who cared either knew, or preferred to learn by looking at the folder.

Since the Depression years the feelings among voters were strongest in 1952, and the 1946 campaign was next strongest.

A tiny few admitted they had voted Republican in 1952 and then had changed their minds. Statistically, some among the substantial number who asserted that they always had voted Democratic must not have told the truth. Some declared support for the Republican incumbent. Not one of the 9,300 said that he or she was for either of my Democratic opponents. One accepted my handshake, folder, and greeting in a neutral, noncommittal manner, then drove away in a truck with an opponent's sticker on its bumper. I smiled and pointed to it as he drove by, and he waved and smiled back.

Many would not look me in the face. Some would say they were too busy to stop. Some would ask what I stood for, as though they expected a speech then and there. A negligible few would ask where I stood on a specified issue. Another few themselves would advocate a measure. Some would refuse to give their names. Others were unfriendly and rude but still willing to tell their names. Some would say, "I voted for you before and you may have my vote this time, too." In the late stages some would say, "It may please you to know that I've already made up my mind to vote for you." While others would say just before turning away, "I've got my candidate picked out, and he isn't you."

Some thought it silly for me to ask to meet them but took a manner of tolerant amusement and willingness to go along with the game. A few thought I was the incumbent. Quite a number, mainly in the suburban shopping districts, thought I was running for the Legislature rather than for Congress. Some would ask, often in a mocking tone, "What are you going to do for us (me)?" A Navy Yard worker on a ferry sneered that if I was elected I never would be back again to see him. At a horse meat market in a Bremerton suburb, a customer said he was a welder by trade and fancied one day maybe he would be a candidate and thereby get some easy work. Out of every three hundred people, about forty would be friendly and one hostile. But the effect of the one to depress or upset would equal the lift from the forty.

A substantial number of older people remembered my father who lived in Seattle for ten years before his death in 1932. If there was any comment it was praise, often with tender and touching recollections of his character, courtesy, and charm. As always, such responses moved me with pride at being his son and discouragement at my inability to capture men's devotion as he had done.

Only a small minority commented on my stand on the issues, either from information received from TV talks or indirectly by word of mouth from others. In the late stages there were many comments on my name familiarity advertising. The TV spots (a clever cartoon) were by far the most often remarked upon, followed by mention of the ads in other media.

Among those recognizable as a class, the most courteous were the persons behind the counter. They treat you as one more customer. The most universally indifferent as a group were the scavengers, the poorest of the poor. Orientals, with a few educated and Americanized exceptions, ran a close second. Among those whom I took to be Jews, not one was indifferent. Negroes sometimes showed indifference, reserved hostility, coldness, and suspicion, but none was deliberately rude. All accepted my hand.

My impression was that some of the hostile and apathetic reactions were not personal to me or to Democrats in general but rather to politicians as such. To these persons politics appeared to represent frustration and futility. They seemed to feel that nothing good can come of politics, that much of their troubles and perplexity is caused by acts and omissions of government, and that they would rather not be reminded of this painful and mysterious fact about which they feel they can do nothing.

In addition to these baffled ones who were unwilling to assume responsibility, there were many others who were annoyed to be bothered about politics. It was not the loss of time they grudged but rather the drastic shift in state of mind. In this aversion to the intrusion of politics they are like combat soldiers who find inadequate their assumption when they enlisted that only others will be killed, and who thus resign themselves to die, preferring the feeling of certainty of a short life to the anxious hope of a long one; or like some shipwrecked persons on a raft who are said to jump overboard when they no longer can endure the doubt about their rescue. This insecure contentment of the soldier in the field is disturbed by talk of long-range plans for civil life, recalling things that he has banished from the surface of his mind, things he wants and fears will be denied him. It revives the problem which he had settled by renouncing one alternative. In this temper, many citizens resemble these men who are too close to death to ignore it as other young folk do.

In a restaurant on Queen Anne Hill, a man seated in a booth talked with me but failed to take my offered hand. I thought him rude until I realized that he was blind. In the same way two deaf mutes unwittingly misled me. On Market Street in the Ballard District, I met a woman who said she had washed my "didies," to use her word, when I was a baby. On the ferry, I met a man with whom I had been a Boy Scout. On Rainier Avenue, I talked with a man who had watched me box an exhibition with Jack Hammer at an Inglewood Golf Club smoker fifteen years before. In front of the campaign headquarters a woman said that she had voted for me last time and then added "in Kittitas County" (150 miles away). On Pacific Avenue in Bremerton, I ran into Bill Whitney who had won a four-round decision from me at Port Gamble. Many of those I met were attractive people of high quality, whom I hoped to have the chance to meet again, and some of whom I wished to know.

Three days after losing the primary, I ran into an acquaintance in the elevator of the building where we both work. He was well dressed and above average in advantages and education. He mentioned that we had met on a street corner about a month before. Then he asked, "Say, how's your campaign coming along?"

When the duty was tedious or frightening during the Second World War, I kept putting one foot in front of the other by recalling words of Marcus Aurelius: "Every moment think steadily as a Roman and a man to do what thou hast in hand with perfect and simple dignity, and feeling of affection and freedom and justice; and to give thyself relief from all other thoughts." In a campaign, under conditions which are comparable but call for less fortitude and more self-propulsion, a candidate may use another precept to keep himself bound to the task. When he has had enough of hunting strangers in the streets and is tempted to take refuge around the corner in solitude with a book or an ice-cream cone, he may think of the remark by Zatopek, the Czech distance runner. Before the 1948 Olympics, other athletes loitered by the playing fields much of the day, available for interviews, but Zatopek would be pulling on his sweat shirt as he stepped out of the car and onto the track around which he then would run for the afternoon. When a persistent reporter came puffing alongside and remonstrated with him for this habit, Zatopek turned his head and replied, "When I come to the track, I run."

Part

Qualities

▼

8

FLAVOR

Citizens' attitudes tend to determine politicians' personality. This determination is made both by the voters' choices among candidates and by politicians conforming themselves to suit their constituents' taste. In time, the kind of politicians' personality which citizens encourage and permit partly decides the direction and execution of our public policies.

A politician's personality has become a substantial condition of his success at winning and holding office. One reason is that our election days are set, not by the swelling pressure of an issue but by the orbit of the earth. In average length, political careers are shortened by the dependence of voters' choices on variable factors of personality, both politicians' and their own. Unlike the situation in most other lines of work, there are no measurable records, such as batting averages, which can be used for comparison, nor does success depend on a consensus among professional colleagues, based on the quality of one's work.

Both historians and citizens have turned their attention away from the politician's personality, meant in the sense of the totality of elements which compose him. Historians concentrate on trends and forces, while citizens give special regard to a politician's "personality," meant in the narrower sense of his flavor to others, the sense in which the word personality is used hereafter. A person's manner is becoming more important and his character less. An air of superiority, though supported by the fact, is thought worse than a lack of superiority. Hypocrisy, because personally offensive, is treated as a worse evil than vice.

In the importance of his personality both for the level of his performance and for the acquisition of rewards, a politician resembles an actor. The professional value of personality as a vendible commodity, and its importance to people and events, tend to make politicians think of their personalities as things apart from themselves, like a tree in the yard. This tendency is emphasized by the egoism of many of the men whom politics, like the theater, attracts. In most professions personality, a bedside manner for instance, supplements one's working skills and colors results. But as with an actor, personality may be a politician's main asset and contribution, his stock in trade which he sells as much as he does his working skills. If he has little from within to contribute he still may make a mark by the impact of his personality. If unconnected with any substantial skill or definite direction in a politician, personality may be a sort of Cheshire cat's smile. To be successful with little inside him a politician has to be in full bodily vigor. But his ideas and character, if he has them, can shine through a frail body with a light of their own.

Now the public eye intrudes into a politician's private affairs, in fact into all he does and is. Modern urban life allows a private citizen to conceal many things about himself from those who know him. But the comprehensive scrutiny fixed on a politician around the clock, by means of technology and custom, makes him feel as though he lives in 1984 and his constituency is Big Brother.

The complete but shallow study of him means that he is known widely but not well. He only halfway feels like the drinker in the cartoon, sobbing to the bartender: "Everybody understands me!" Information about him comes at second hand, and he is observed only while engaged in his never-ending courtship of his observers. Before impressions of him reach the citizen, they are filtered through an interpreting medium such as a news reporter's mind, modified by the editor's mind, or a TV screen, altered by technicians and producers. Even when seen in the flesh he has his guard up. There is no way to know how much of a prepared speech originated in his mind, how far his brain and mouth may serve as a mere transmission belt for others' thoughts.

American society now asks for one of certain general personality types in its politicians. With its detailed but imperfect knowledge of a politician's nature and activities it verifies the degree to which his performance complies with its request. A politician used to be known largely, and therefore judged, by his work and his conduct in connection with it. Those who dealt with him in person, his colleagues and opponents, were the ones who took his measure. Now there is less tolerance of nonconforming natures. It is not enough that one acts right; one must have the correct personality as well. If he wishes, a private citizen can disregard in part the public's gentle, pervasive command, but a politician must obey it to be preferred and thus to survive. At his peril he bucks this tide. He must keep Stendhal's words in mind that "The approval of others is a certificate of resemblance." Success in politics today, subject to the condition of an acceptable personality type, would be almost as hard for some of the Adams family titans as for the tigers on the Assyrian throne.

Among the elements of the preferred personality type are moderation, sincerity, and warmth. None is essential. La Guardia was immoderate; Dewey and Robert Taft were not warm; politeness and the wish to avoid partisanship forbid me to give examples of those who have substituted earnestness for sincerity.

The distinction between warmth and coldness of personality is superficial as to human nature and invalid as to morals. Many men conceal strong appetites and passions beneath layers of defense. Their manner betrays, not the important quality of indifference to life, but the minor one of a habit of caution, or distaste for a show of feeling. The meaning of outer warmth, not a virtue but a personal attraction, has been perverted and inflated by popular tastes and falsified by today's deliberate conviviality. A cold fish may be sensitive and good. In politics, the most warmhearted lodge brother is not worth a Wilson, a Hughes, or a William of Orange.

One can classify mankind better than as the faucets on a tub. A division can be made into three classes, one composed of animals, the second composed of persons who, as their own judges, make decisions after balancing the merits of the consequences, and the third composed of those who commit themselves to follow certain moral rules. The members of the first class pretend that anarchy exists and obey society's rules only so far as is necessary to their immediate personal interest, while those in the second and third classes have loyalties and good intentions toward persons and principles beyond themselves. A person in the second class treats all norms as issues in equity where the factors must be balanced so that a sacrifice is not made without some compensating gain. A person in the third class regards certain rules of conduct as laws having only rare exceptions, so that he will take a risk for a principle or person without counting the cost. Holmes's soldier is an example: ". . . the faith is true and adorable which leads a soldier to throw away his life in obedience to a blindly accepted duty, in a cause which he little understands, in a plan of campaign of which he has no notion, under tactics of which he does not see the use." Other examples are the choice Lee made between the Union and Virginia, and the refusal of the Secretary of State to turn his back on his fallen friend. Not all the members of the third class are superior to the second, because the third contains some whose otherwise admirable natures are tarnished by timid or cruel rigidity.

The current preference for warmth over virtue has the same root as the preference for sincerity over honesty. Sincerity, the identity between one's tastes and feelings and one's expression of them, is one of several kinds of honesty, which is the identity between one's expression and the thing to which it refers. Friendship depends on honesty but cannot survive without occasional insincerity. Chinese and Russian Communist leaders tend in their behavior as such to be sincere but dishonest. Lord Chesterfield's code of conduct, based on policy and honor, enjoined him to constant honesty and frequent insincerity. Both sincerity and warmth improve a personal relationship. Honesty and virtue do not.

While directness of purpose and capacity for superior work are, as always, the main assets required for reaching the top, the lack of inherited gifts of rank and circumstance is being replaced as a barrier to political success by the lack of moderation, sincerity, and warmth. The latter makes political 4F's of some men and women who as politicians would do public good. The decline in the importance of party organization has made it easier for a man to succeed in politics without the skills of working with an organization, yet it has made it harder for him to overcome the absence of the vendible elements of personality. He has to get along with everyone because it is no longer enough to get along with fellow party members alone. One result is to admit to office politicians who have energy, ability, and charm, yet lack purpose about anything beyond their own careers. Leo Durocher said about big league baseball, "Nice guys finish last," but in politics they often finish first.

However, there are trends afoot which may restrict these limiting factors and put the luxurious virtue of individuality within a politician's reach. The growing recognition of the narrow limits or even nonexistence of a man's power over his fundamental elements and thus his responsibility for them has extended to those aspects of personal appearance, beliefs, and conduct, including moral choice and strength, which are due to family, race, or custom. The result is an increasing tolerance for those whose difference is the evident result of ancestry, religion, or national background.

As part of our tradition, behavior is allowed more latitude than belief is. There is more truth to the myth of rugged individualism as to conduct than as to thought. But although people are no longer described as weaklings or sinners or lesser breeds without the law, intolerance yet remains for habits and beliefs which appear to be outside or counter to a person's background and which deviate from current popular taste. The realization that who and what we are is largely determined by causes outside us has not yet spread to apply to those habits and beliefs. They still are thought to be exclusively a person's own so that he can be blamed for them. Because they do not seem to be determined by heredity or environment they are treated as free will's final redoubt.

This residual intolerance is reinforced by the lack of a widespread wish to be allowed this kind of independence for oneself. Everyone wants to escape the pains and burdens of race or religious prejudice, or to avoid punishment for a crime committed pursuant to an emotional disorder, and most people are willing to see the burial of such a sword which can be used against as well as by them. But the desire to enjoy individuality is confined to a minority now. The fear of loneliness if one does not conform denies sympathy for nonconformists. The lack of humility about the possible rightness of others' deviations and lack of confidence in, and respect for, one's own conforming practices make nonconformity appear to threaten and insult one's own beliefs and ways. This intolerance is due, not to certainty of being right, but rather to misgivings about whether one is right and a feeling that no one else knows enough to justify himself in differing from the crowd.

Most people in time may come to regard a person's "voluntary" singularity as having been shaped by his background as much as were his flat feet or his choice of fish on Fridays. In this event voters would permit and, unless their toleration slackens to the point of indifference, might even prefer the presence of independent ideas and character among politicians. However, even if people cease to blame a person for his nonconformity, they still may suppress it for the general good as they would any tendency thought to be harmful to mankind.

The suppression of nonconformity may be stopped by two things: understanding and respect. Understanding of personal peculiarities may spread to the sources of nonconformity and relieve the fear and suspicion of it by removing its mystery. This understanding of other people is going far. It may become the main cause of the conditions which will "save succeeding generations from the scourge of war." Toward that end national boundaries are tending to embrace ever larger sets of diverse groups which formerly went armed against each other. Understanding may in time conquer much, if not all. Once it exists, a sympathetic understanding does not easily stop at encompassing a portion only of its object. In the Leyte campaign our anti-aircraft fire hit the solitary Japanese plane which came overhead on Christmas night. I felt a tender pity for the pilot far from home as he and his plane blazed in the sky like a great star.

Popular aversion to nonconformity may also be reduced by increased respect for it. Before long every man may have many of the freedoms of a king. These new conditions may generate a taste for certain of the old values which resulted from aristocratic ways. Among them is the individual's importance. In recent years individuality and self-respect, like good manners, have tended to be scorned by many people who resent these qualities because they identify them with a haughty privileged class. When Harold Hoshino, a prize fighter, was boxing a convict as part of a show in the prison yard, one of the crowd shouted, "Knock him out, Pete, he eats ham and eggs!" As the memory of unjust privilege fades, most citizens may come to tolerate expression of a strange idea even when it remains a mystery or continues to be detested. When the suppression of nonconformity has declined until it remains only in the form of the gentle but enveloping weight of public opinion, independent behavior may then increase, as people come to realize that when everyone is tolerant of them they can get away with a lot. Yet some in the advance guard of attitudes now admire tolerance and understanding more than insistence on the rightness of one's own principles. Confusing righteousness with self-righteousness, they hold a pukka sahib in lower regard than they do a squaw man.

In order to represent his constituents well a politician must embody much of what they believe and like, but his duty to give his constituency responsive representation is not violated by his having a mind of his own. He may bow down to brazen idols, or, like Kipling's Lascar seaman, he may worship a low-pressure cylinder, although he may not be a monarchist or advocate the system of a single tax. In matters that concern public policy about which his constituents have definite opinions he may not deviate from the norms of the moment as far as a private person is free to do, but he may keep a consistent purpose supported by a firm character.

To be in accord with the consensus of his constituents' policy wishes does not require him to be a conformist any more than antagonism to them makes him an individualist. Tolerance of individuality or of a direct aim in a politician does not mean indifference to what he stands for but rather acceptance of the independence of his outlook. A leader, to lead, must be independent but not eccentric. If he is an extreme nonconformist he tends to lack sympathy for his constituents and cannot inspire their trust. But if he conforms to the point of letting others make all the decisions about his course he does not lead. He may help people get what they want but he does not help them discover what else better there may be to want.

As Erich Fromm has written: "The right to express our thoughts, however, means something only if we are able to have thoughts of our own." Free speech has little worth to those with nothing to declare except what they receive from others and then transmit intact as though they had not even looked into the box in which it came. When Evers used to take the ball from Tinker and throw it on to Chance, at least he changed its course. Citizens gain only from a politician who gives them something of himself, who transforms experience as it passes through him, who is not a mirror but a prism.

When his freighter was torpedoed near Greenland, my friend Fred Sundt jumped into the lifeboat, where he discovered that the rest had done the same, and so there was no one left on deck to lower the boat. If there is no one left for a politician to follow, he may as well lead. He may try to assert, rather than suppress, his independent ideas if he himself is bored by his pattern of affable blandness, if he feels a duty to exercise leadership more far-reaching than hunch bets on next month's opinion polls, and if he is encouraged by an increased public taste for more original fare. As in the case of customers for bread, citizens defeat themselves when they put excessive emphasis on how their politicians taste, because in time they receive a flavorless product.

9

MODERATION

This chapter is about three kinds of moderation: in policy, in manner, and in character.

Moderation of *policy*—forbearance from extremes, a temperate approach to inflammatory problems, the use of reason which is sometimes detached, an attempt to delay action during heated periods so that reason may be applied before important measures of policy are taken—is essential to the practice of free government but of little use for its achievement or defense. Its value is to keep the conditions in which free government can flourish. Because free institutions are maintained by moderate policies and acquired and protected by immoderate ones, they depend on politicians who have a preference for moderate over immoderate policies but the capacity and willingness to use either when needed. In times of stress, when moderation is inadequate, an adequate politician is willing and able to be immoderate toward the end of moderate government, which in the long run depends on a sometimes fighting faith.

The notion that a politician who has a mild *manner* cannot or will not be tough when the public interest so requires is a folly common to dogmatic fogies of the left and right. This notion is unfair because it is untrue. A person can use violence when he thinks it fitting even though he is humble, reserved, or dignified, like Joe Louis and Robert E. Lee. Often soft-voiced politicians in subdued dress have brought their country into war. Because Benjamin Franklin, prosperous, rational, and habitually temperate, wished to be allowed to continue to be so, and because he had courage as well, he was willing to stake all on revolt. Those people who fail to distinguish between a mild manner and a slack or rigid character think that a person whose approach to problems is tentative and thorough is therefore spineless or a fossil. They have scorned mild-mannered politicians as craven for not using as their guide the New Deal after it had been embalmed, ratified by the Republicans. But any manner, mild or otherwise, in a politician can be compatible with a belief in freedom and the courage and force to act on such belief.

Moderation as a quality of a politician's *character* has been practiced to perfection until it is a curse. Gibbon deplored immoderation in public affairs as a major source of harm:

"In the tumult of civil discord the laws of society lose their force, and their place is seldom supplied by those of humanity. The ardor of contention, the pride of victory, the despair of success, the memory of past injuries, and the fear of future dangers, all contribute to inflame the mind and to silence the voice of pity. From such motives almost every page of history has been stained with civil blood."

But we now are choked with sympathy and smothered in forbearance. Modern politicians have become too moderate in all aspects of conduct and value except narrowness of purpose and willingness to do hard work. Forgetting the limits which bound the golden mean theory, they treat it as a universal, like the candidate for mayor who promised to tread the line between partiality and impartiality. To put it another way, they fail to apply the theory to itself and so they practice moderation to excess. They try to be only moderately wise and brave, like well-to-do college boys who used to think it vulgar to become learned and aimed to get a "gentleman's C."

Free government depends on a type of politician whose character is equipped for both smooth and rough going. He can handle the daily low-tension problems with a restrained hand, yet his preference for life in a free climate is so strong that in order to restore it if it is lost or to defend it if it comes under fire, from

within or without, he is willing to kill or die. His balance does
not leave him stalled at dead center on an occasion calling for
immoderation, whether such occasion be a radical reform to hammer through or an invasion to repulse. A Communist, for example, is unfit for this task because he has none but the martial
virtues—courage and loyalty to the authority which he obeys. He
lacks the temper to operate free institutions and the inclination
to make them his goal. Even if he cared about freedom he would
be useless for its practice. Such was the history of some Resistance fighters against the Nazi rule, first in war but last in peace.

Among those American politicians who cannot perform this
dual function the only common type is neither an obstinate reactionary nor a zealous absolutist. It is a politician whose whole
nature, not merely his manner, is so moderate that he can behave
in no other way. With his moderate attachment to constitutional
liberty, this type is a fair-weather boat.

The predominance of this type is preferable, however, to the
condition of some unstable democracies where extremes attract
most of the support, leaving a weak center, so that the shape of
politics resembles a dumbbell. The American pattern of classes,
based on talent, and the pattern of political outlook among politicians and their constituents both seem to be shaping into the
form of a fat middle with tapering extremes. This desirable form
is itself unstable unless the persons who compose the bulk of it
have courage and some conviction to supplement their open
minds.

Tacitus wrote of Agricola: "It was a case of a lofty and aspiring
soul craving with more eagerness than caution the beauty and
splendor of great and glorious renown. But it soon was mellowed
by reason and experience, and he retained from his learning that
most difficult of lessons—moderation." Several conditions cause
this moderation of character, which is no longer difficult to learn.
In the field of managing affairs, although mobility of status has
increased, there is less risk of disaster or chance for supreme
eminence. Enlarged opportunity has lifted the limits of achieve-

ment in certain fields, as admission of Negroes to competition
has raised the levels of supremacy in music and athletics, and the
increase in the proportion of scholarship students has pushed up
the average quality of honor graduates. But as to status and
power, as distinguished from achievement, the range has narrowed between ordinary failure and success. The floor has risen
and the ceiling dropped. How many politicians now seem to make
their secret motto: "Aut Caesar, aut nihil"? Desperate effort is
no longer called for by ambition or fear. The struggle has abated
as we have grown more tame.

Another cause, growing in strength, is the complexity of social
organization and the need for highly trained minds which are required to operate it. Within both organization and minds the
paths of action are obstructed by screens, blocks, settling basins,
corners, and red and amber lights. The effect is to raise the
threshold for intemperate and sudden action.

Another cause of the new moderation is the effort to improve
the adjustment between the individual and society, an effort
made by persons both as members of a group in respect to other
persons and as individuals toward the group. If every citizen were
on harmonious terms with himself, politics would be a more attractive occupation than it is because a politician would not be
afflicted by the corroded souls who now give him much grief. But
if every one is going to be so well-adjusted to society that he is
contented with it, few may hear a call to enter such a single-
minded life as politics. Winston Churchill has observed:

"It is said that famous men are usually the product of unhappy childhood. The stern compression of circumstances, the twinges of adver-
sity, the spur of slights and taunts in early years, are needed to evoke
that ruthless fixity of purpose and tenacious mother-wit without which
great actions are seldom accomplished."

More than ever, the politician's attention is fixed, exclusively
but not intensely, on his relationships with his constituents,
rather than on history, posterity, or God. The shift of attention
is partly due to the constituents' new power and to the respect

to which they have become entitled for their own worth. No longer a mob, "a great beast," most of them now are educated and disciplined in the practices of citizenship. The term "public servant," once less fact than blend of self-serving deception and polite ideal, has become an accurate label. But increases in life expectancy and in self-awareness are the chief causes of this increased attention to personal relationships, which in turn is the strongest cause of excessively moderate character.

In the past when a person spent his life in the shadow of death he was more aware of the power of chance and the supernatural, and he thought about an afterlife. He knew neither philosophic doubt nor economic hope. We now tend to feel assured of the use and enjoyment of our allotted span. We know that there has come to pass a chance to enjoy true and sustained happiness on earth. People have forgotten they are going to die. Death has been hidden from our sight. Only undertakers touch or care for bodies, which are taken promptly from the place of death. Brief ceremonies for the dead are held in a commercial parlor instead of in the building which was one of the central places of the mourners' lives. Evidence is lacking that widows no longer honor their husbands' memories or sooner cease to miss them, yet now the period for wearing black is short. Like sex in the Victorian Age, death has become unmentionable except by a euphemism. Its discussion is shunned, and its existence concealed from children.

Our concealment of death from ourselves takes away our sense of the tragedy. When we not only remove from our presence the horror of a corpse, but draw a curtain between ourselves and all aspects of death, resulting ignorance leads us to underestimate the level of that highest plane on which life can be taken. Years ago, near where I was working on a farm, a lad climbed on the freight train as it passed each afternoon and rode it half a mile to the pasture where he would jump off and drive in the milk cows. Once, when he made the mistake of grabbing for a rear ladder instead of a front one, he missed and fell between the cars, and the wheels ran over his thighs. A man who had seen him fall got off his horse, pulled him a few yards up the hillside, and got a doctor, who tied off the bleeding and gave him an injection to numb the pain. The lad could see his house from where he rested on the bunch grass. He looked across alfalfa fields to the burnt hills, to the green timbered slopes behind them, and to the snow peaks on the horizon under the fall sky. He smoked as his family and his nearby friends came to stand around him. Little was said, but the living and dying exchanged goodbyes. When he was dead his brothers took his body into the house.

Longer life expectancy has raised life's value by raising death's price, which is reckoned by the lost years of life's expected remainder. A soldier, once he has a mortal wound, has no more chance to make himself a hero. The life of Pertinax compels our admiration, but not because when he died at sixty-seven he faced his assassins calmly and did not try to hide or flee. The same goes for Abraham Holmes, who amputated his own arm after the battle of Sedgemoor. During the Bloody Assizes he was brought before the King, who gave him the choice to recant or hang. "I am an aged man," he said, "and what remains to me of life is not worth a falsehood or a baseness. I have always been a Republican, and I am so still." At seventy, when Socrates and Seneca drank their hemlock with dignity becoming to the elevation of their lives, they proved their wisdom rather than their courage. It is said that when a weather-beaten soldier of Caesar's guards came to ask leave to kill himself, Caesar, noticing his withered body and decrepitude, replied, "You fancy, then, that you are yet alive."

A result of the probability that one will reach old age is to make a politician less independent of his constituents, more cautious, less reckless with his life, more inclined to make long-range plans for himself and wait patiently to harvest them, less willing to start a war, less willing to play for high, immediate stakes. And in this attitude his constituents back him up. So far as politics is a game of chance it might be expected to lose appeal except that the consolation prizes have improved.

The assumption of carnal immortality makes man seem even

more important and centers the politician's attention on the people, judged by their own standards. There is little thought of eternity in time or space except among a few who may reflect on some of their kind setting out for Alpha Centauri on a journey several generations long.

Politicians' average age may be expected to rise with that of the rest of the population. This change, combined with increased life expectancy, may increase the proportion of politicians who are moderate in character and raise the degree of their moderation. In policy, this moderation of character among old men tends to take the form of conservatism as in the case of European politicians after the World Wars, when the younger men were dead. T. E. Lawrence wrote: "When we had achieved, and the new world dawned, the old men came out again and took from us our victory and remade it in the image of the former world they knew." On the other hand, if older voters feel less need to treat a politician as a father image, a larger proportion of women and younger men might be elected, and thus the spread in age by which politicians exceed the average of their constituents would shrink. Also, the number of beats allotted to each heart is being increased more than is the span of capacity for hard work. A person can pull the levers on a voting machine a score of years after he has lost the power to give effective service as a politician. There are men who may have cast a vote for both Washington and Lincoln and others for both Grant and Eisenhower, but when they voted last they could not do much more than blink their eyes and state a simple choice.

The increase in man's self-awareness has become so great that it can be classified as a difference in kind. All men, not merely philosophers, now know man to be the measure of all things. His double nature has long been recognized. Walt Whitman said that animals do not lie awake at night and weep over their sins, and Chesterton said you cannot slap a rhinoceros on the back and tell him to pull himself together and be a rhinoceros. But we have acquired a paralyzing knowledge of the degree to which our subterranean selves govern our motives and conduct.

Another cause of self-awareness is our uncertainty about values. This uncertainty makes it difficult or meaningless for a person to pass an objective judgment on another person or a human situation. So he considers his experience of the other person or the impact of the other's personality or conduct on his own feelings. Instead of judging others he tastes them.

Now it is hard for an educated person to yield to emotion or act on an emotional conviction. When a feeling starts to surge inside him he can hardly help thinking of the effect of the emotional process on himself, thereby altering the quality of his emotion and reducing its force. When my father came to tell us children that grandfather was dead, he sat down, put his face in his hands and cried. I wonder how my sons and daughters will inform their children of my death. Perhaps their sorrow will make them start to cry. In turn they may be reminded that tears are a healthy catharsis. The comfort of this gain may stop the tears. People used to go to church to worship God. Now when people kneel some remember that prayer is thought to be a therapy. In such self-regard one cannot pray; God goes unworshiped, and the supplicant goes without his cure. If it is taken as medicine, and with knowledge that it is a placebo at that, the Host becomes just another biscuit.

In our well-ordered society, politicians, like most other people, have lost some of their former dependence on friends for favor, protection, and hospitality, although congenial company is important for politicians' pleasure. Added to this decline in the value of friendship as a means of survival, the new self-awareness has weakened a politician's loyalty to and affection for friends; it also impairs the quality of his loyalty to institutions. A person's inclination to do something for another's benefit is retarded by his knowledge that he is impelled by some irrational frailty within.

Another effect of this self-awareness is to make it easier for a person to commit small sins but more difficult for him to commit big sins. When tempted to do a minor evil act he expects the consequences to be "guilt feelings." This prospect of a personal affliction like a stomach-ache is a shallow bar to sin compared to the former stern and heavy sense of duty to do right. On the other hand, before committing some dark, ferocious deed a man reflects that the source of his intent is a thwarted impulse. Its satisfaction does not seem to be ordained by the Infinite. Its misdirection may be corrected. It seems hardly worth the certainty of anxiety and the risk of punishment. He remembers that the offensive conduct of the prospective victim is due to his unfortunately twisted soul. At this point, a man will put away his gun, shrug his shoulders and look up a psychiatrist or take a pill. To tranquilize, instead of exercise, his longing for revenge seems more easy, sane, and safe. The result is to diminish the intensity and violence of moral decisions, whether good or bad. Less often does a man become a brute or a martyred saint.

In addition, this awareness checks the pursuit of distant goals by denying a refuge in illusions. The result is fewer drastic and uncalculated enterprises, a skepticism toward effort to achieve what seems to be impossible, fewer great endeavors to win "the true glory," "that good fame without which glory's but a tavern song." We are emancipated from our passions without embracing reason, as we disdain the one but distrust the other. If we insist on truth we cannot wish for illusions to beguile us. But the conscious loss of illusions makes people shy away from ideals which they mistake for more illusions. When some people said that John Brown had thrown away his life, Thoreau questioned where they had thrown their lives. Like a race of Sancho Panzas in a world they never would have made themselves, today most persons hesitate to shoot the works.

We may be in for a long period during which man cannot possess himself, cannot merge his two selves, cannot put down his looking glass. Our public leaders may tend to be artificial in their displays of passion or conviction. They may be more reflective, less ready to adopt a hypothesis for radical change.

People have come to look deeper in placing responsibility for human acts. At first the offending thing itself was blamed. The ox in Exodus was to be stoned. Then the act's effect and the actor's identity were the only things considered. Later the question of criminal intent came to matter. Then the motive behind the intent. Now investigators go hand over hand far back along the chains of cause and effect in search of the sources of conduct. If the first three Gospels were being written now, the authors would not think to call the men who were crucified with Jesus "thieves."

It is coming to be thought that human actions are the product of genes and experience and therefore not a proper subject for either praise or blame. Moral responsibility is narrowed to a necessary fiction. People understand all, and so forgive all. Moral qualities are treated less as universal norms and more as building blocks in the construction of personality. Now security, equality, and prosperity are making every one an actor who can pick his part, and create it from diverse elements. Just about the time that we are forgiving every one his total personality as being the product of causes beyond him, we invent means by which he can conceal his background and fabricate his personality by altering the details that compose his appearance and flavor to others. There is release from the moral rules which were embodied in traditions and in the need to make a living, rules which have been only partially replaced by the duties of citizenship in its broad sense. Aware that they are free to manipulate their own personalities, politicians may assume such virtues as they choose. But these qualities are more likely to resemble items of taste than obedience to iron commands from On High. This expanded freedom of choice is exercised in a manner tempered by the growing doubt that a person is the godlike originator of his acts, despite his power to look at the sky and read his destiny in patterns made by celestial bodies which he himself in less than seven days may have constructed in a shop—and despite his share in mankind's choice of making planet Earth resemble either Heaven or the Moon.

On certain idealists in politics the effects of self-awareness have been incomplete. A man of this kind holds tight to his independence in order to escape the risk of turning into an oppor-

tunist who scorns and follows his fellow men. He reminds
himself to be detached and humble to avoid the mad belief of
thinking himself destined to command. He keeps his high principles but may come to cherish his integrity as a pearl of greater
price than worth, just as the value of any gift can be exaggerated
when treated as an independent end.

These factors are changing politicians' mental habits less now
than those of their constituents because politicians, inclined this
way by their profession's emphasis on shifting personal relationships, were affected first. Three centuries ago Dryden observed
that "Politicians neither love nor hate."

For ages, wise men have warned against the folly of soft blows
and shrewd men have avoided them. Machiavelli observed that
failure to conciliate or destroy enemies was to court loss of office
at least. Emerson reminded the young Holmes, who had shown
him an essay on Plato, that "When you strike at a king you must
kill him." When the Samnites had surrounded the Roman army,
they could have put it to the sword or magnanimously set it free.
Instead, they let it go after leading it under a yoke as a gesture
of disgrace. The army marched back to Rome, smarting for the
revenge which in time it took.

But in dealings with each other political enemies have grown
less hostile, less capable of great harm, and less susceptible to
be won over as trusted friends. One's antagonists—even the word
"enemy" is too strong to be accurate—are less often individuals
than groups. A politician no longer can deal with an opponent
as though he were a wild animal. For a politician to destroy an
opponent is a function which modern ways have made as out of
date as for a businessman to ruin a competitor. Now halfway
measures are the sensible and customary course. And halfway
measures have become composed of persistent, smiling pressure,
instead of blows which wound but do not kill.

People have a softer shell and a more impermeable core than
they once had. Despite their closer surface contact with each
other, their relationships are seldom deeply intimate or ardent. Of
those who now make personal relationships the central aspect of

their work many come no more to grips with other people than did those persons in the past whose attention was fixed on the ideas or things which were the subjects of their work. After a slight acquaintance people tend to address each other by their given names, and thus erase gradations of familiarity. By going in the same direction, all people now are coming to resemble politicians in these attitudes. Citizen and politician may give each other greater sympathy because they share some of the same problems and experiences resulting from a multitude of superficial relationships. The diminishing difference of attitude between politician and private citizen and the merger of the politician's functions with those of business and military leaders, making the subject matter of their work more alike, are giving them an even closer similarity of outlook. Politicians' present attitudes are being adopted by other leaders and by Everyman as well.

Now politics and private life are not so far apart, and a politician's mental adjustment is relatively slight in passing back or forth. The transition in and out of marriage is an example of a similar trend. Young single people tend to pair off in temporary partnerships which are more like marriage than the former free exchange of companions. With easy divorce, the commitment to marriage is less final. The distance between the single and married states has narrowed, and the step across is less abrupt.

The modern American politician has the qualities of caution, discretion, tolerance, and moderation. He need not be as ruthless as his Asiatic counterpart must be today. Nations are shifting from war to other means to get their way. In politics there is a similar decline in the use of tooth and claw. Personal ties are bent but rarely broken. Elastic negotiators take the place of implacable foes. In contrast to the Emperor Otho, "who acted the slave to make himself the master," a modern politician is a good fellow both before and after election day. In character and attitude he is almost the antithesis of those mailed and clanking knights of the Crusades who fought for God, for glory, and for fun.

10

HONESTY

At the same time, technology and science have increased the harm done the public by a politician's lie and reduced the harm of a politician's theft. A politician rarely is diverted from the path of right by pursuit of immoral pleasure or illegal gain. His weaknesses take other forms. Standards of money honesty are higher than in business because making money is not such a compelling motive among politicians and a larger proportion of their financial transactions is subject to public scrutiny. One does not enter politics if his chief aim is to get money for nothing, or even for something.

Money honesty in politics is less important than it was. Society is richer, so it more easily can afford some loss by theft. There is less temptation to steal, and less theft now, than when it was harder to earn a good living by working for it, and before thorough record keeping and efficient law enforcement methods increased the odds of being detected. The penalties are not as severe as in the past, but one still is ruined if caught.

A politician has several ways to steal: to take bribes, to take from the public treasury, to extort money from subordinates whom he has the power to fire, to pocket the excess of campaign contributions over sums spent, and to engage in speculative trading based on his knowledge of future governmental acts. None of these crimes but the last, which is detectable in other ways, can be committed without the help of other people, whose knowledge increases the risk of his being caught, and whose apprehensions tend to deter them from taking part, and thus make it difficult for the politician to find his indispensable accomplice. Like illegal gambling, the principal vice of money dishonesty is its degradation of public officials and the consequent loss of confidence in government.

▼

The great moral problem of American politicians is intellectual honesty. A free society cannot operate unless leaders tell the truth to the led, and when they cease to be honest with each other as well the fabric of organized society tends to dissolve. For the wheels to turn, words have to be trusted. Life is too short for every statement to be put on paper before a notary and under oath. Montaigne wrote, "We are not men, nor have other tie upon one another, but by our word." Although average levels of honesty among men are higher than ever before, the public need for it from politicians has grown further than the standards of practice have risen.

Among politicians there are three means of deceit: promises, charges of crime, and the substitution of pleasing diversions for truth. Failure to keep a campaign promise is not a serious wrong where it is due to the difference between capacity and hopes. But to assure a result in the knowledge that it is unattainable is a fraud. An example is to promise in the same breath a balanced budget, lower taxes, full employment, and armed forces strong enough to dismay our enemies.

In the name of patriotism, some leaders in and out of government abuse their power and the leverage of the public trust by accusing people of crimes they did not commit. Such were the charges that China was given away and that Dean Acheson and George Marshall were patrons of traitors. In addition to the wrong suffered by the victims, these injuries done as official acts shake public faith in our government's justice.

The third form of dishonesty is to use the methods of group suggestion to instill false beliefs. This form of deceit is practiced and permitted about vital subjects involving deep emotions in areas of thought where people are easily misled. An example is the use of slogans which are substitutes for policy or masks for lack of policy. One slogan is picked up when the last wears thin, as in jumping from log to log across a mill pond. The fault is not in the use of symbols but in their falsity. The system is to lull or excite fears, hammer on plausible fictions until they seem true, and omit important facts. Its purpose and effect are to make people think that problems have been solved when they have not, or to make them content with what is, instead of demanding and expecting solutions. The result is to deny citizens the understanding they need in order to pass the judgments which are an essential part of the democratic process. In the past, leaders tried to solve public problems, even though with a class bias. Now there is the tendency to let a problem lie and induce the citizens to think it does not exist or that things are better as they are. In case of a fresh water shortage, instead of trying to convert salt water to fresh, the preference would be to convince people that the sea has the better taste. In contrast to psychiatry's aim of enabling a person to rid himself of misconceptions about his personal life, this governmental method *supplies* illusions about public affairs.

Some of the persons concerned with the private morals of the public feared that the Kinsey reports would corrupt those people who confuse the meanings of "is" and "ought." This lazy equation is part of the philosophy of power for its own sake, the belief that might is right. The advertising and public relations agencies have been among its chief institutional exponents. They treat national problems as soap to be sold rather than knots to be untied. They handle the issues of employment and peace in the way they push the sales of ointment to make hair come off or oil to make it come in. These would-be fathers of mankind betray their scorn for others, whom they choose to mold as pliant lumps rather than to address as free men who can understand the truth.

Stalin called intellectual leaders "engineers of human souls." The risk is the acceptance of this concept and its adoption as a principle of government, that is, the substitution of "positive thinking" for thought, the use of mass media and organization to shape each person into a docile, uniform, and well-adjusted member of society and keep him that way; the attempt to determine, not the truth of a proposition, but its appeal to the psychic needs of the audience. People are gently guided as one blows a toy sailboat in a basin. By these means a national or world-wide state could be governed perpetually and without change by a single group of experts without an army or police. This oligarch's paradise would in theory, and possibly in fact, be impossible to overthrow. Brainwashed from birth, a man would be denied even the modest privilege of martyrdom.

The fatherly manipulators would be a self-perpetuating body like the board of a mutual insurance company. Bertrand Russell wrote, "If you control the police it gives you the godlike power of *making truth.*" Control of the police is merely the initial means to control of the media and the educational system, which can instill whatever the ruling group chooses to label as the truth. All it takes to put this over is the apparatus of mass suggestion and freedom from honest principle. Already, the mass media cling to the common denominator and shut out dissenting voices. De Tocqueville wrote that before the Revolution "France had not yet become the land of dumb conformity it is now; though political freedom was far to seek, a man could still raise his voice and count on its echoes being widely heard." An unpopular or unknown idea now receives an insufficient hearing through the media, which provide the only substantial audience. Free speech remains, but it is so weak that it has become freedom of whisper or freedom to shout into an unconnected mike. Many of the men engaged in making taste and opinion, except for a few old-fashioned publishers, so dread being disliked that they would be willing even to tell the truth in trade for love, but there is no sign that many people dislike them for their deceit.

Not only have we acquired the means for large-scale manipulation but we have become more susceptible to these means.

The growing taste for entertainment in politics and education may soften resistance to being deluded while amused, because when we are entertained we tend to enjoy, or at least not to mind, being fooled.

Yet government of the many by the few would not be a one-way street for long, because the few would become conditioned by their own methods of control. In the past, thought and immediate power were separate. The training of manhood for violent force excluded thought, while beyond a point cultivation of the mind made one less willing to face a gleam of steel. It is said that when the Goths were sacking Greece they decided not to burn the libraries because they thought that reading books would keep the Greeks from the practice of arms. Now, for a group to be strong and effective its decisions must be made by persons who think. The men who have the skills to make and use dreadful weapons, to handle big organizations and suggest taste and action to the multitude, all think. Their own routines, propensities, and values inhibit them from bloodshed and coercion. The most powerful Americans of today have been produced by a training system which would never make a Mucius Scaevola or a Blackfoot chief. Absolute control at first might be attained by hard-boiled gangs. But the nature of the work is such that their members would become, or be succeeded by, affable and sympathetic types engrossed in their relationships with others. Hardly anyone has strength enough to combine ruthlessness with sensitive concern for others' tastes and wishes. Desires and thoughts would be passed back and forth between the many and the few, and altered by each group during passage of a circuit. The few would cease to be operators of an engine, and would become influential players in a serious game. They would deal with the many as a chess expert takes on several men at once, each move he makes being partly determined by the preceding moves of his opponents. Like advertising writers who prefer to reflect rather than improve the grammar of their audience, these men would conform themselves to others as much as they would mold them.

By insensible steps, mankind would become a single group dynamics club, at peace and perhaps happy but in a partial dream. As to what might happen after that I dare not speculate.

This trend toward winning favor by reciprocal deceit has the safety for us of being conspicuous. If the worst comes, it may be some other evil. After a while perhaps the pragmatists will recognize honesty's value in their own terms. There may be enough people who so much want to keep their minds their own that they will bring about restrictions on the large-scale means to manipulate personality, just as the weapons of mass destruction are going to be controlled. Intrepid skeptics guard against invasion of our minds. There are more among us than is apparent, because those who cannot talk well or do not care to talk fail to reveal their defenses to a selling pitch. However, among persons who proclaim their doubt of the authorities, those who think cynicism a more sophisticated pose than enthusiasm are guided easily by suggestion toward unreasoned beliefs.

Problems too big to be avoided by pretending their nonexistence provide another limit to this dangerous trend. To hurdle such a problem a politician requires skills for more than manipulating the masses and public support for his efforts to solve it. Public participation and consent cannot be obtained for sacrifice unless the people are told the bad news. When at last the facts reach them through the layers of quilting which have been put around them, the people tend to replace politicians who fail either to be realistic in meeting those problems which cannot be exorcised or to be truthful in telling people about them.

Churchill wrote that in 1940, at the end of the day when he had been appointed Prime Minister, as the concentrated might of German arms descended on his island, he lay down to dreamless sleep because "Facts are better than dreams." The question is, will there be enough people who prefer facts to dreams who will stand up to this trend and reverse it in their finest hour?

To increase this vital number what should be done by honest men? A condition of honesty is the practice of rationality. In this uncertain day when answers are so hard to find, the pendulum first has swung far toward determinism and authority, and many have sought shelter in some absolutist creed; now it has been swinging to the other end of its arc, an uneasy agnosticism and unwillingness to be committed. Much faith in rationality will be required for us to steer a course between the comfortable absolutes of ignorance and truth. But "our prejudices are our mistresses; reason is at best our wife, very often heard indeed, but seldom minded." Using the reason that we have, we may shape the malleable and irrational elements of men's minds in such ways as to enable them to make best use of their powers of reason so that they can be honest.

The subrational premises in people's thought used to be instilled by their parents. Part of this responsibility is shifting to public agencies. Their problems are: how to enable children to discover the wisest diversity of choice and to have the best chance for experiment with what they are to believe and be when they grow up, and at the same time to impart to them the discipline and knowledge which have been acquired and accumulated by those who have gone before them; how best to reach the children who now receive much of their moral guidance from the media and from their peers; and how to teach children to give and take the truth?

Because children are people, and so not exclusively rational, they cannot be brought up on the assumption that they will cleave to the truth when they grow up merely so long as they have not been misled in childhood. They cannot be vacuum-packed until maturity. To try to do nothing but develop their powers of reason is to allow children to pick up their absolute beliefs at random from their experience of the world. When Chief Justice Vinson wrote, in the case of Dennis vs. U.S., "Nothing is more certain in modern society than the principle that there are no absolutes," he declared a drastic absolute. To teach children that there are none is to make the same mistake. To the extent that schools are to share responsibility for the moral upbringing of children, what shall be stamped into children's minds? If nothing, then except for extracurricular information, the children will grow up heathen, not even pagans, having heard of neither agnosticism nor God. If something, then what? Is it bad for them to be heathen? Our problem is not avoided by the constitutional separation of church and state, because whatever is or is not taught to children will tend to shape their moral attitudes, and because much can be done in moral, not religious, training without transgressing the bar.

Some people believe that to indoctrinate an enclosing framework of absolutes like Communism or Catholicism is to establish the necessary order within which one can be free. But persons who think that such dogmas make it harder for a child to approach the truth merely refuse to face the problem if they pretend that no absolute beliefs should be implanted in children's minds. It is a necessity, not a duty. The question is not whether but what, because it is impossible not to instill some basic attitudes by act or omission. Politicians are soon to meet this problem's impact in helping parents to decide the moral values which the public grade schools are to teach. In the days when the basis for morality (why be good) was agreed to be conscience or the church, such authoritative reason used to be a proper absolute fed to children. But in many quarters now there is less certainty about it. Perhaps a substantial proportion of the people in the future will agree on a philosophic basis for morality, but I see no imperative that there be agreement except on the practical matter of uniform public policies. To reflect and preserve the diversity of our national society in our effort to produce honest citizens it might be well for us to have the schools proceed on the humble assumption that we do not know which of us, if any, has the Absolute Truth, but that truth exists and ought to be respected and pursued; that the schools forbear to indoctrinate any divine or practical grounds for morality; that they teach children certain first principles, and when the children grow older teach them how to doubt these principles if they choose; and that without an effort to explain they instill in children the honesty, skepticism, loyalty, and love, which are essential to a society of free men.

One means to solve some aspects of this problem would be to adopt a system of elementary and high schools less directly controlled by the public than the present system. Each school district, assisted by funds from the U. S. Government, would provide a minimum school fee for each child. The fee would be uniform for each age level, with adjustments depending on the local cost of living. The district and government would accredit private schools that conformed to minimum intellectual and moral standards, as was done under the G.I. Bill of Rights, and that did not discriminate in unreasonable ways, such as according to race. There would be compulsory attendance, as now, but free choice of school. Competition among schools to attract pupils by producing children trained to get along well in the world would make for some conformity to the world's values. But such a system would bring about more diversity of approach in education and a greater chance to combine the search for truth with the training of the young.

11

BOREDOM

The failure of communication between citizen and politician disappoints many people who feel that something has gone wrong. But this communication has never been good, and it used to be worse. Only now has it become a recognized evil because in the past the leaders did not care and the people did not hope. Citizens are frustrated rather than resigned because they feel that the failure is not inevitable, that the obstacles can be removed. Wishing understanding and appreciation from their constituents, politicians are anxious about their lack of sympathy. Most politicians have acquired an emotional dependence on the people because they need them, respect them, deal closely with them, and no longer have the reassuring knowledge that the people are vicariously living through politicians their glories and their comforts.

This failure of communication is not due to lack of information which citizen and politician receive about each other. Such information is more complete and accurate than it used to be. As in the case of communication between churches and their congregations, the vital matters which fail to be communicated relate rather to significance and purpose; the meaning of the political process is not communicated. The failure of communication between citizen and politician is largely due to the unreality of politics which in turn is both result and cause of its dullness.

For the effective communication which is necessary for a free society there must be understanding between the parties. This understanding depends on political engagement to the extent of participation by some and attention by most.

Many people make themselves do their citizenship chores by will power based on an often exaggerated, and currently declining, sense of duty. They detest and shun political engagement because they feel it is a boring, far-off business and they resent their obligation. Citizens feel they are not players, but only spectators or victims, and that the process of government leaves them out. Moral entreaties are not effective to get people to vote, and voting is insufficient participation either to satisfy the citizen or serve the need of the state. There is no hope to breed in men the sense of civic duty of Aristides or Brandeis. Among those few on whom such effort is successful some are unable to do and understand what they have been made to feel they ought. Beyond a point, exhortation in this direction does no more than generate indifference and guilt. Yet political engagement, because an essential condition of good government, is a duty, as joining the union is for a person in a union shop. To refuse to take part is to secede from the community. Our purpose in this matter, as in much of public policy, is to make good conduct appealing enough to be practiced. If the political truth were to be more artistically communicated to citizens, thereby making politics more real, people would less unwillingly turn to politics. A healthier climate would result from a sane and less grudging approach.

The subject of citizen participation, beyond casting votes, need not be national or international affairs, although most people know these things are important. Some people who feel strongly about issues on a wider scene think they should be able to influence, or at least understand, events there and feel frustrated if they do not have the chance. Some think local politics trivial and vulgar, and that nothing short of nuclear weapons control deserves their attention. The main concerns of others are the transit system and pollution at the swimming beach. Issues are available for every taste.

The problem is the manner in which one takes part. Routine measures of actual participation, such as handing out hortatory leaflets, can satisfy only a few. The shift of the campaign process from party organization to media has left amateurs little significant work. Energetic study which contributes nothing except to the improvement of the student is unsatisfactory to most people. Like other complicated matters not absorbed through normal experience, public affairs require effort to understand, and useful political engagement is possible only with understanding. The effort of study may nevertheless be made if other aspects of involvement are made entertaining in the manner of other optional enterprises requiring effort yet giving enough pleasure to induce the effort, such as crossword puzzles, bridge, and climbing a hill to see the view from the top.

Political engagement is essential not only to active citizen contributions to the public good but also to communication, the more essential element of the democratic system. As engagement by citizens can become a satisfying experience only where citizen and politician truly come in touch, the converse also is a fact; successful communication can be established only where citizens can be brought by the offer of satisfying experience into some degree of engagement.

After taking care of their necessities of existence, people now have time left in which to give politics the attention which it needs. Their choice depends on whether politics offers them the pleasures that they want. Politics no longer has much attraction for citizens in terms of compensation for service. Partial political engagement for the chance of jobs or fees appeals to few. It is not needed to guarantee security from private persons or from capricious governmental acts. Nor is it needed to hold or obtain a substantial class advantage. Therefore, politics can appeal to citizens for their attention and participation mainly to the extent that it can offer pleasing or satisfying experience rather than protection or contractual rewards for what they have done.

People have become less dependent on politics for entertainment but more dependent on entertainment everywhere to satisfy their wishes. In their attitude toward politics the mass of people used to be passive because, having little power, they felt they might as well relax and enjoy the stately processions with their banners, embroidered clothes, polished metal, and nodding plumes.

Now for new reasons people want politics to be entertaining as a condition of their attention or activity. They want this despite their present political power with its solemn duties, despite the fact that they are more literate and better informed, and despite their lack of dependence on politics as a major source of entertainment. Memory remains of the tradition that politics provides amusement. In some ways people have acquired more of the outlook of the guest or customer, whose function is not to act and to decide but to receive, consume, and be entertained. A taste for pleasure is the main cause for this demand. People have developed more cultivated tastes for entertainment, so that their capacity for its enjoyment is increased. Parables and funny stories no longer will suffice. People have acquired the opportunity to obtain frequent pleasure, and most of them have chosen it long enough to make a habit of this choice. They prefer to spend most of their comparatively pleasant lives in the enjoyment of pleasure. Depending on the individual, the pleasure's nature and level vary. It may be his sole end, his chief end, or an incidental accompaniment to some other satisfaction. He may take it as actor or spectator. He insists only on a course of experience which entertains enough to please.

Political engagement can be obtained from people only if politicians furnish pleasing experience. For people to be induced to take part or at least to pay attention they must be amused. Entertainment of certain kinds increases understanding both by direct effect and through citizen engagement, of which amusement is a condition.

If politics were not so dull for voters, politicians, to get attention to their words and themselves, would not have to resort to superlatives and noise. People are bored by a politician before he opens his mouth. Rare is the political speaker whose "look drew audience and attention still as Night," like that of Milton's Beelzebub. Flamboyance is not enough. Access to superior art and entertainment is no longer limited to a small group. Passive recreation is popular and excellent. Adult work and play are mixed.

Like the schools, politicians have to submit to the condition that their pronouncements be fun if the audience is to listen. (Yet compared with some teachers, politicians have it soft. In New Haven I coached boxing at the Dixwell Avenue Community House; in Seattle I conducted a Bible class at the Cathedral of St. Mark. No political situation has been as hard to meet as these tests of teaching adolescent boys.) Those persons with an attitude that all experience must be sugared expect a politician, like a teacher, to compete with professionals whose skill is specialized and high and whose performances, unlike his, are not diluted by such frequent commercials.

In communicating the truth in politics, art is needed to give amusement as well as direct understanding. This amusement can and should be furnished on all levels of drama, humor, and beauty. Serious obstacles to creating this element of amusement have been raised by the changed functions of entertainment in politics and the distraction of other amusing things.

Once a major source of entertainment for the public, politics has become a small sideshow with loud barkers but unexciting acts. Required to deal with a populace which was ignorant of public issues and whose political power was small and largely negative, leaders used to practice calculated pageantry in order to maintain a passive consent to the leadership and to turn attention from, rather than toward, public questions, as now. Later, as most people began to acquire political power, entertainment was used to obtain their approval and choice. As the people still were largely uninformed about public affairs and not yet inhibited by the "pale cast of thought," leaders approached them largely through superficial appeals. Bonfires, free liquor, and bombast were combined in order to please and arouse. It is said that in the back country of Ghana the campaigns consist largely of arguments about the relative merits, as persons, of the elephant and the lion, which are the symbols of the major parties. Until now it has been fairly easy for politicians to amuse people because there was less attempt to inject a discussion of issues and because people had little amusement available to them other than to watch a hanging or listen to a speech. Old people who were enchanted long ago when a circus came to town are puzzled when their grandchildren take the circus as a matter of course.

Politicians now find it harder to be amusing than they did before. They have to tell people about serious problems which the people have to decide. Educated for utility instead of pleasure, they are unskilled in the arts of amusing by their speech. They fail to attain even the level of declamatory rhetoric. Part of their failure to amuse is due to the lack of attention given even to utility in their education for language and speech. The schools have shifted emphasis from the art of communication to other things. Furthermore, the language has been debased and it has been rapidly altered and stretched to meet new conditions. One reason why politicians are less amusing is that they are unable to use the tools of language to communicate well because of the decline in both the fitness of the tools and politicians' skill in their use.

A candidate used to be able to develop and improve an important speech by practice, repeating it before many small audiences. For three years before he carried away the 1896 Convention with his "Cross of Gold" speech, Bryan had been giving it in the Mississippi Valley. Now a politician's speech is heard by most interested listeners the first time. This difference resembles that between plays performed live in a theater and over television as a one shot performance. The talks a candidate now gives to small groups in a campaign are largely small talk rather than a discussion of the main issues, which are saved for the broadcasts.

The professional entertainers have risen in entertainment skills, while politicians have declined. Judged as entertainment, politics now is inferior to good professional entertainment, using the broadest meaning of the term, whether the common label of the producers is entertainer or artist, whether the product is boffolas or beauty. The size and profits of the entertainment field have increased; specialization has concentrated in this field most of those who have a talent to amuse. If they had lived a hundred years ago probably a number of the best contemporary entertainers would have entered politics or the ministry instead.

Some people regard as distressing evidence of their fellow citizens' moral decay the fact that politicians have low audience ratings in comparison with Toscanini, Bob Hope, or pictures of naked women. Although our moral fiber may be growing slack, this popular preference is no proof of such a trend. It used to be no more entertaining to watch a juggler juggle fruit than to watch a magnificent cardinal conduct a mass or to watch a duke in a warm and handsome suit astride his horse. But now, because it is better entertainment, professional entertainment is more diverting than politics to most persons who are not participants in politics.

The unreality of politics, causing failure of communication, is increased by the distractions of both professional entertainment and self-amusement such as boats and books. Politics seems more unreal when it is so dull that it can attract little attention. The most powerful diversion of attention from politics is professional entertainment through the mass media, where politics and entertainment directly compete. The media affect people's political attitudes in two ways: through their use by politicians and others on the subject of public affairs; and through entertainment, which affects politics not only by diverting attention from it but by shaping attitudes toward it.

Although his constituents wish to be entertained, for a politician to amuse them with wit or humor is dangerous as well as difficult. Wit and humor help to hold an audience until it hears the things one has to say, and ridicule is sometimes useful as a club. However, a funny person may be dismissed as a clown; many people equate humor with lack of the dignity which most people demand for all public offices except a few vestigial ones. In the latter they enjoy a jester only because they can afford him. Wit may win a politician grateful applause from a bored audience, as it used to do for Mayor Jimmy Walker, who once was introduced at the ground-breaking ceremony for a subway tunnel after a long-winded speech by another man. Walker stepped forward and spoke one sentence: "You build a subway with a pickax, not a thorax." Then he started to dig. But wit suggests the brilliance many think incompatible with sound judgment, which most people prefer in their public men. A caustic wit may be thought ill-tempered, and an intellectual wit may be thought high-hat. A politician is likely to be hurt no matter whom he makes the target of his wit. If he turns it on himself, people may believe the truth of his playful self-criticism, instead of applauding his humility. In heated controversy it is hard to hold in check a single item of one's verbal arsenal, and bystanders may be worried when a politician's wit is used to scourge another's folly. Bacon wrote: "He that hath a satirical vein, as he maketh others afraid of his wit, so he had need be afraid of others' memory." As in any mass communication, a subtle wit will not do. Common denominators of expression forbid things meant to be recognized by a happy few.

Politics is likely to become flabby and stagnant unless politicians find some way to entertain their constituents. "Weight without lustre is lead." It will not work to forsake entertainment as too difficult and to try instead to impress by transmitting the image one wants to present. This course entails only a fleeting contact with the people, not a continuing involvement of them. To mix politics and entertainment does not in itself do harm. Entertainment in connection with politics can be used either to supply illusions and distract attention from the facts or to give a deeper understanding, both by obtaining attention and by the use of beauty as a path toward truth.

A politician should try to entertain, although it is impossible for him to compete effectively on their own terms with the professional producers of drama, beauty, and humor, and it is unnecessary for him to try. Instead of competing with his superiors in the field of conventional entertainment, a politician can better reach his audience by making politics, through himself, more real. To do this requires art.

The use of art in politics and political communication is not a novelty. As he was about to return from Egypt, Shaw's Caesar declared that Rome appreciated art. An elegant Sicilian sneered that the only art enjoyed by uncouth Rome was what it bought or took from others. Caesar replied, "Is peace not an art? Is war not an art? Is government not an art? Is civilization not an art? All these we give you in exchange for a few ornaments. You will have the best of the bargain." As an artist's attention swings between his audience and the vision in his mind, so a politician's thinking oscillates between his constituents and his policies. Much art of all kinds affects political attitudes in ways which are pronounced, though hard to perceive, and even harder to measure. Aldous Huxley once advanced the notion that a substantial cause of Germany's political instability was the absence of the novel as an indigenous art form. Wagner's music is thought by some to have encouraged the acceptance of Naziism. Except in Calvinism and Communism, beauty has been used by organized religions to win and hold adherents. The increased importance of entertainment in American society more than ever has given power to the writers of the country's songs over the content of its laws.

As an artistic supplement to the educational and politically deliberative processes, art may be used, by politicians and others, to transmit the truth. A politician's purpose in his use of art is fourfold: to give understanding of the truth directly by making the communication more intelligible; to amuse and thereby attract attention to it so that it will be noticed and deciphered; by pleasing, to encourage participation, some of which is a condition of politicians' being understood; and to shape public attitudes toward politics and politicians' personalities in ways to make politics more real.

Politicians can diminish the unreality of politics by forbearing to flatten their individuality and by approaching utopian goals; that is, by means of identity and ideals. "The environment of the twentieth century," wrote Barbara Ward Jackson, "is designed for the men who dare greatly and dream greatly and let their work catch up with their dreams."

Public acceptance of a wider latitude of personality among politicians would permit a larger proportion of politicians with a distinct identity to exist as such. It would reduce the requirement that a person either be a dull politician or stay out of politics. The proportions of character and ideas in politicians could be increased as a supplement to ability and a substitute for moderation and warmth. Most valuable would be those politicians who incorporate the elements of independence and purpose, who contribute more of themselves, advancing ideas which they did not necessarily originate but which they chose. Because each detail of politics is dull unless it is regarded as a means to some splendid end, independent politicians with direction of their own inject into politics a sense of adventure, the tingle of statesmanship.

Our anxiety, which in America now seems to be endemic, is due more to the absence of appealing paths of aspiration than to the lack of a ceiling on some kinds of competitive effort. Our discontent is caused less from trying to scale a greasy pole of infinite height than from the absence from our sight of any poles which we think worth a try to climb. Universal leisure intensifies, and largely creates, the need for new ideals. Even guided leisure is not an adequate substitute for ideals since it provides artificial temporary goals but is aimless in the long run. The politician who assumes the role of the games director at a resort fails to fulfill the people's need for goals. Aimlessness, whether applied to leisure or to work, is a dull doctrine for a politician to expound.

The need for utopian goals is most evident as well as immedi-

ate in the case of bringing up children. Nowadays the lives of
their parents appear to children in some ways as they did before
the industrial and social revolutions. In the intervening period
the children of each generation were given to expect adult lives
on a higher level of comfort and civil liberty than that of their
parents. Before that era, children could look forward to living on
about the same such level as their parents. Now too a child knows
he will dwell in a house like his parents' house. But the incentive
and expectation of effort to rise above one's parents' levels of comfort and civil liberty have declined, and the set of rules arising
from the facts of life in an earlier day which provided evident
goals for both self-interest and benevolence has weakened. Then
one had an incentive to work hard in order to live more comfort-
ably, and in order to be kind and generous to the unfortunate.
Now few people are unfortunate, and their misfortunes are largely
taken care of by institutions. So what can a child aspire to except
to be a good citizen so that the institutions will be efficient and
just? He is not given narrow roads bounded by limits to his activity. He is not given norms of duty such as to be loyal or to
work. He has no clear conception of his role, what it is to be a
man. Why should he learn to be gallant to women who are as
self-sufficient as he? Why should he be taught physical courage
if he is not to exercise it beyond the playing fields, if drugs protect
him from pain, if police protect him from attack by individuals,
and if he is to learn that each country's military force is like a
scorpion in a bottle with the others? Is there any good reason why
this child ought not be like those despised tribes of old whose
valor had been eroded by prosperity until their cups were heavier
than their swords? Should parents teach their children that the
end of life is retirement after college?

   Once wooden ships made iron men, but modern circumstances
are so kind they do not help to impose character on a man. He
gets little more than what he contributes by his own efforts which
are generated at the command of voices from within or without
him. We have a special need for men who will put a sharp edge

on themselves so that they will be men. Now that the necessities
of survival are weaker forces to drive men to strenuous action,
men's action depends more on the voices to which they listen,
independent of necessities. In the past men collided with circumstances through their efforts to master or avoid them. Circumstances were like a spinning grindstone against which a person
had only to lean in order to acquire an edge. Now that conditions
of life are easier, the softer circumstances will have to be hit
harder than before to raise a bump. They are more like a whet-
stone, requiring active effort from us in order that we may become
sharp. The edge can be acquired from the same collisions as formerly, but the inner effort will have to be more strenuous than
was the previous effort, which was impelled by necessities of survival. If we treat as force (which equals mass times acceleration)
definiteness of character, that is, willingness to follow voices calling for an independent course, which may be a collision course
with some other persons and ideas; and if we treat ourselves and
circumstances as mass, then as circumstances become lighter we
can obtain sharpness of character only by increasing the acceleration with which we hurl ourselves against circumstances.

The old ideals of dignity, comfort, and justice, largely after-
thoughts forced on us by indignity, hunger, and inequality, may
be replaced by new ideals which represent more of a free choice
than a lash. As ideals, these may be more important than the old
ones were because the old ones had to share their force, often
most of it, with fears and appetites. But with fears, both rational
and irrational, abated and appetites satisfied, the new ideals may
tend to operate alone in shaping mankind's course.

To improve communication a duty lies on each side: on the
part of the people to permit politicians to be individuals; and on
the part of the politicians to take advantage of this opportunity
and to proclaim utopian goals. A politician bores his observers
and fails to reach them if, like a poor musical composition, he has
no direction and if he lacks a theme which from time to time
he can restate.

12

AN ARSENAL OF CIVIC ASSETS

Here is a catalogue of those virtues, skills, and attitudes which an American politician needs in the second half of the twentieth century in order better to lead a government of free men. The possessor of all these assets is the answer to a good citizen's prayer and would fit the terms of a convention nominating speech. Some of our politicians have many of them in a high degree, so this ideal does not insult the real. Although some of these characteristics may help a politician toward success either through personal satisfaction or through rewards from others, the common element of the items on this list is that they enable him to do good works. This chapter is not concerned with success as such, even though success in terms of greater power, whether through ability or situation, may better enable one to do good works.

Some knowledge of history is needed for a politician to understand government, and a sense of history is essential for him to avoid living only in the present and therefore assuming either that his own epoch is eternal or that it is easy to transform. Without a sense of history he lacks the standard of judgment which can protect him from measures which are excessively radical (Does he know how many ideal commonwealths have been brought to pass by slaughter of leaders or enactment of a new code of laws?) or reactionary (Will he be like the trembling purchasers of full-page ads proclaiming that forty days remained in which to save their country's way of life?).

Toward the same end of perspective, he needs an inner life with a system of principles for his direction. This is both important and rare. The intensity of contemporary stresses makes some sensitive and thoughtful persons crack up or turn inward, leaving the field to nimble men who are directed by ambition and the pleasure of their peers rather than by any more permanent rules. They are undented by the forces to which they yield, unaware of the strains and indifferent to the public good. To be wiser and more effective, a politician has to take pains to be a whole man. To keep an outlook of freedom and wide horizons, he must do three things: At intervals, he must take time for reflection under conditions of peace and leisure; he must have a few friends who care neither about politics nor about his personal success; and he must practice some diversion remote from his work. Unless he exists as a distinct person he cannot be much use to others or much pleasure to himself.

From Moses to Nehru, few statesmen have struggled to success and had a broad and long conception of the world who did not first pass through a period of forced and painful solitude in adult life. This element of growth is harder to acquire in the United States than abroad in conjunction with success of a kind which depends on concentrated activity. One who stops to reflect may not catch up, and if he does resume the challenge round of competition he needs an excuse for his quiet time, such as an attack of polio, to save him from rejection as being odd.

In the course of a political career several returns to private life will disorder a politician's routine but at the same time offer him a chance to give better service when he is in office. The result is to follow two careers, practiced in alternation, one public and one private. The advantage of these sojourns, which do not have to be in obscurity but should be free from pressure, is the chance to acquire a better comprehension of the present by giving attention to the past and future. A politician is better able to understand and contend with the present if he does not live in it continually. In office, a politician's reading time is short, and almost all his study is consumed by periodicals and technical reports because he must concentrate on immediate problems. Life is too short to allow him at the same time to bolt each day's raw facts and to digest information and conclusions about long periods. The exceptions, such as Churchill and Theodore Roosevelt, are too few to matter. A philosopher politician is a personality of which I cannot conceive and for which I therefore cannot hope. But a politician enabled by periods of tranquillity to improve his sense of the past and future and his own identity is both possible and to be desired.

A sense of history, an inner life, and periods free from responsibility for daily decisions, all tend to give a politician a sounder judgment in his decisions, and they tend to make his policies moderate and more definite and realistic in direction. A person who remains in the commotion of dealing with daily problems cannot be committed to anything but action for its own sake or a temporary survival on other people's terms. One can be aloof without ever being committed, but one cannot become committed to any significant end without from time to time being aloof.

▼

Shaw said that democracy is a device which insures that people are governed no better than they deserve. Whether they are is no business of a politician. He has no right to say to people, as though he were a fireman standing with his hose and looking at a burning house outside the city limits, "Everything I give you beyond this point is beyond my duty and puts you in debt to me." A deserving constituency should get a politician whose ego is in close balance, with that self-esteem which a man must have to act with his full force, yet without the notion that he is at the center of the universe, a notion which distorts a man's judgment and morals by fixing his eyes on himself. He has a will to win, but curbs his thirst for glory and crusading spirit to permit the detachment necessary to act in a way that is wise and good. Justice Holmes wrote: "A man is bound to be parochial in his practice—to give his life, and if necessary his death, for the place where he has his roots. But his thinking should be cosmopolitan and detached. He should be able to criticize what he reveres and loves." This politician does not enter a suicide pact with a lost cause, but will submit to humble compromise to trade a halfway measure for half a loaf. His attitude contrasts with the adolescent martyrdom of one who suffers total defeat by inflexible devotion to his plan because he puts his pride or self-pity above his conception of the public interest, while pretending to put principle first, pretending he would rather be right than useful, though in political terms he is not even right.

This imagined superior politician's own mind directs his acts, yet like most men he is a political animal, not a member of a more solitary species, like the great cats. The public opinion polls are not his compass needle. His constituents influence but do not own him. He does not think he is the Great White Father Figure leading the scorned masses beside the still waters of social security. He may prefer three cheers to three meals, but he is immune to that pernicious disease which attacks an otherwise able leader whose outlook is immature and woolly: first worshiping the cheering crowd; then, as he sees himself reflected in their eyes, coming to believe himself the proper object of their worship. As a free man he does his duty as his brother's keeper by enabling his fellows to be free.

▼

A politician should be able to reach a decision and stick to it long enough for the people whom he affects to act on it. The process of compromise is a constructive element of democratic government only if a politician interrupts it at recurring intervals and steers a straight line which enables other people to take directed action. Otherwise they cannot know where they stand or what is practical or safe to do. Whether his problem is a budget, a foreign aid plan, or a zoning code, a politician should know when to halt deliberation and fix his course. Only if others can count on him to hold fast once in a while can they proceed in reference to him, get up speed, and make some distance before his course is changed again. That part of government touched by a politician stagnates if he never ceases to alter his position according to the moment-by-moment resolution of forces upon each other and upon him.

To do justice, government has to combine certainty, requiring consistent policy, with adjustment to clashing interests and shifting conditions requiring, respectively, compromise and change. A politician ought to alternate between a sensitive responsiveness to changing needs and wishes and a firm course with a measurable bearing and rate.

▼

A politician gives better service if his loyalties are divided and if they are graded in order of their importance to the public interest. If he has no loyalties he is useless. If his loyalties are in the wrong order he is less useful than he could be. If his loyalty is attached to a single object he is likely to do harm. His first preference should be to his principles and to all the people to whom his unit of government is responsible. This group should rank above his constituency if the two are not identical, that is, if his constituency is a part of the whole, as is the case for most legislators except city councilmen elected at large. If he loves his policies as himself he may ignore their defects and continue to cling to them after they have become obsolete. On the other hand, the public interest suffers if his friends come first. But for his decisions to be untouched by friendship impairs his service. The supporters of such a politician may be fewer in number, and therefore as a unit less effective in his cause, than the group surrounding a politician who cares enough about his friends to stand by them to some extent. At the same time this smaller group of supporters is composed of a larger than normal proportion of fanatic types who adhere to him, not from affection but from devotion to his policies and devotion to him for his attachment to his policies. Their backing and counsel tend to warp his judgment.

▼

As a support or substitute for character in politicians, a moderate ambition has value which a voter should not scorn. It makes a man assume some virtues which he lacks. An ambitious politician knows that his practice of them does more to advance or support his success than mere verbal tributes to good. He knows that honesty is a good policy. The wish for future trust and recognition restrains him from selfish excesses and spurs him to work. Unless he has superior strength of character, a politician without hope of some reward beyond that which inheres in virtue is likely to be dangerous or useless. As a marriage can be held together by character in the absence of love, so by moderate ambition in the place of character the commonwealth can be assisted, if not sustained.

▼

A politician ought to be a teacher. Powers of advocacy are not enough because they cause only a superficial persuasion, not enduring understanding. By eloquence, you can carry people away against their better judgment some of the time. By teaching, you make them harder to fool. If you are a better man than your opponents, you need not worry. Mr. Truman's conduct of the Presidency suffered from his lack of teaching skill. Some of his best proposals failed because he was unable to convince the American people of their worth.

Some politicians ignore their teaching function and do not try to exercise it, but, regardless of intention or awareness, all teach by character and conduct, if not interpretation of ideas. A politician can teach even better than schoolteachers those things which are within his experience. As broker between government and people, he explains public problems to citizens. Their comprehension may enable them better to form the basic policy which

is passed back to him to be translated into legislation or administration. His teaching assists his constituents, his country, and
himself. If people understand what he is about, they may be more
willing to support him. This is particularly important where he
acts for the welfare of a unit broader than his constituency or a
special interest group within it. People may know what they like,
but a politician can help them learn their long-range wants.

▼

The value of intelligence and education in politicians is more
clearly recognized than some people realize. The danger of the
mob's dictatorship is mitigated by organized society's need for
brains. In the past, although intelligence was required for ad-
vances in knowledge, what it took to make the world go round
was a combination of capacity to lead, force of character, fortitude and valor. Now the world must have first-rate minds and
will pay for them with almost all the rewards for which an intelligent man may ask. The spread of education and the abolition of
unpopular privilege are tending to reduce popular hostility to
trained minds and to evident brains, hostility caused by an
identification with hereditary privilege and by the love of equality
running riot. Many people in the advance guard of thought are
overly pessimistic, however, because they do not appreciate the
prospects for further decline in fear of learning as the masses free
themselves from ancient superstition to the degree that their
leaders have done. As the mystery disappears, the fear and awe
tend to be replaced by respect, although the scorn for disinterested intelligence does not seem to be abating at the same rate, if
at all. Politicians will continue to deal with scientific matters
which the masses will not understand, but a politician will not
be resented for these arcana because they will be no more com-
prehended by him than by any other people who are not scientists;
he merely will use them, knowing something of what they can
do but not how they work.

▼

Imagination is an important quality in a politician. In public affairs, all things under the sun have been tied together in a web
of cause and effect. Not long ago, if a politician could understand what was before his eyes and within his experience, he could
handle his job. It stood within these horizons. Now his mind must
see the sparrow fall in a far-off land and know its effect on his
constituents.

In one type of public man vision is short, although his sight
is clear in the cozy, brightly lit cell of his philosophy. He sees
government in terms of administrative competence and the balance sheet. Another type sees it in terms of each man's dignity,
singularity, and capacity to exceed himself. One bases policy on
hopes, the other on regrets. As a symbol of political outlook a
rainbow is better than a ledger. Politics needs both.

A politician need not be an original thinker, but a new idea
should not make him flinch. In proposals for action, his thought
need be only just far enough ahead of his time to be within the
understanding of his constituents, yet beyond their natural vision.
Any more is a dangerous adornment of little use to him, while to
fall short keeps him from being a leader, although he may be a
success. If he should come to believe the wisdom of some advanced idea for action he should keep it to himself until the time
comes, if ever, when he may advocate it without making many of
his listeners angry, bewildered, or afraid. He ought to propose an
attainable end, one to which the voters probably can be per-
suaded to go, not one to which they would move their affairs if
only they could be induced to agree with him. When Solon was
asked if he had left the Athenians the best laws that could be
given, he replied, "The best they could receive."

A free government requires that some of its politicians be willing to try new ideas. A disadvantage of intellectually mature politicians is that many of them are indifferent to new ideas for
action, even though unafraid of them. A mature politician's free-

dom from illusions about the nature of the world is often coupled with a reluctance to experiment because he doubts whether a proposed change of course will work or do good. Among mature politicians this common distaste for trying new ideas is partly inherent in maturity and partly the result of the fact that to obtain mature politicians people tend to elect old ones; age and maturity combined accentuate the preference for habitual patterns. Like the golden mean, the ideal of philosopher kings has limits. Old, mature men who have lost passion, vigor, and illusions, tend to be not only temperate and sensible but also bound by a taste for the tried and, so far, true.

A politician should be able to combine his measures for immediate action with a glimpse of a long-range goal. The "conquest of space" is one target that may be erected. In logic this phrase, which calls on us to dominate infinity, is of course absurd. And yet if taken as a direction, one which is not to apply to any sapient beings whom we might meet in outer space, and to whom we would not wish to play the conquistador, this phrase seems merely presumptuous, like every admirable aim. After all, a worthy challenge to the human race may be to conquer something which it cannot even comprehend. When a politician points to far-off realms of gold, he must not fail to make it clear that he is aiming at ideals, not calling for immediate action; that he is urging a course or a change of course, not a running jump into the distance. He may and should hold up a star for his constituents, but he has to leave no doubt that it is a long way from his and their wagon.

He dare not propose, or even reveal that he foresees, a state of things which contradicts the hates or fears of the moment, such as friendly equality with some current enemy race or creed. For example, Isaiah safely prophesied that "the leopard shall lie down with the kid," but an American politician during World War II could not predict that shortly his constituents' sons would be bringing home brides from Japan, and in some states a politician would as soon lie down with a leopard as foresee that the races will mix.

A useful end for him to urge is a tentative ideal pattern for society. This is not to propose a single step ahead of the existing path of progress, it is not to recommend another car in each garage or nonstop flights to Tahiti but a whole new framework for a way of life. Only by this means can people be enabled to evaluate their present way and, if they find it wanting, to decide on the best alternative target. For a long time, political talkers have been chewing a stale cud. In America politicians now are needed who will spell out brighter, better worlds and show us roads for their approach.

But regardless of the end proposed, whether a far-off comprehensive scheme or the location of a bridge, the politician should take a stand, not confine himself to fearless endorsements of completed public works or praise of great dead men, or pronouncements like the Aztec lords' annual vow to keep the sun on its course. Otherwise, he is worth little to his constituents, and politics is not worth its cost to him.

In personal terms the price of political success is so high, and knowledge is so uncertain about its causes, that you might as well enjoy yourself by taking sides. It is not necessary that your convictions be strong. Nor do your stands have to be consistent, either in sequence on one subject or on several subjects at once. And of course you need not take a stand on every issue. But you must stand up for something in order to exist separate from the abstraction of mankind, and to be a man. Of the Spartan kings at Thermopylae, Demaratus lived longer, but most people ever since would rather have been Leonidas.

At the proper time and place, a politician has the duty to discuss with his constituents every item of policy in his program. But although he should propose utopian public ends, he is wise to say nothing of the lifetime goals he has set for himself. It is presumptuous to think anyone is much interested in them, and they may prove embarrassing. He has to take more pains to keep the remnants of his privacy than one whose daily life is less exposed. He need not affect beliefs he lacks, like Henry of Navarre who decided Paris was worth a mass, but taste and discretion bid him to contain those almost inexpressible thoughts. His ultimate, unattainable ends, if he has any, are properly revealed by his conduct.

▼

If a politician's great problem of self-restraint is to forbear to mold his fellow men, and to forbear to mold himself to suit them, his high duty of positive effort is to be brave. Conditions of modern leadership narrow opportunity for physical courage and reduce its value, although it has far from become a dead asset, like a natural immunity to smallpox. But under today's uncertain, thunderheaded sky it is more important than ever, as well as harder than it used to be, to let our minds be bold, to act on independent judgment, and to live by principles, especially one's own. We forget the unceasing dependence of freedom on courage. In some ways bravery was easier in days of old when there were dragons into which you could stick your sword and an audience to applaud. To struggle bravely with formless masses of society is like swimming in the middle of a gentle tropic sea. For this perplexing time when courage seems either futile or unnecessary we can recall the words Pericles spoke at the burial of Athenian dead, "The secret of happiness is freedom, and the secret of freedom is a brave heart."

Unless a politician's courage is exercised as an act of responsibility, it is at most an indirect assistance to the cause of freedom or the commonwealth. The public good need not be a motive. Nor does it matter whether the nature of his action is combative zest, the nerve to confront a danger in order to escape it, or willingness to risk a loss for chance of gain. But the public good is not served unless his intent is the defense of a principle, a policy, or at least a portion of the public. Bravery for one's family is a private virtue. If his aim is merely to win elections, a politician's willingness to stand up to angry crowds is gambler's nerve which proves his ambition rather than his public spirit.

Of all brave efforts which contribute to the general good, the ones of highest value are those efforts which a politician makes when he declares the truth, and next most valuable are those he makes when he fulfills his word. Veracity most helps the cause of freedom at those times when veracity depends on courage. And courage as an element of probity inspires less folly than courage does in other forms. Even where the public welfare is a politician's conscious aim in exposing himself to harm, the public does not gain by it when his action is misled by narcissistic motives supplemental to the motive of the common good. The memory of Marcus Curtius was honored for his having caused improvement of his city's central square, whose beauty and convenience were impaired by a gulf, which closed as soon as he had galloped into it on his horse. But evidence of the price which divine forces had set for their performance of this piece of public work was thin enough to suggest that substantial elements of his decision were excessive pride and a pleasure in self-display.

Yet for a politician the problem is not solved by any kind of bravery alone. To serve the public interest, or the cause of freedom, virtue cannot be coupled with continual defeat. Popular admiration for success encourages belief in the morals practiced by winners; people often despise the high principles for which a loser stood. If he makes a gallant losing fight, the crowd will cheer him when he leaves the ring, but next week it will go to watch the other fellow fight. Many candidates are pragmatists about the ethics of what it takes to win, yet primitives in their assumption, with inconclusive proof, of a causal connection between methods and elections. If a man has been elected after dodging issues or defaming his opponent, he and others will perform the beastly ritual again.

A politician's basic task is to draw the line between the public interest and his own survival. It can be claimed that this continual decision is not moral but strategic, that it is a matter of judgment alone because except in office politicians cannot do much public good. This would be so if man were just a scale. But his judgment is distorted by his hunger for success. Idealism and good sense may cause him to identify his country's fortune with his own, but then, deluded by conceit, he sees their major causal sequence in reverse. He must have courage to speak about the important things with more honesty than his judgment suggests. Discretion is not worth as much as valor. As he follows the line between truth and success he needs courage to favor the former.

Furthermore, an aspiring mankind should have men and women willing to risk their rank to save their honor. To be a politician of a democratic nation, one no longer needs to risk his property or life. The public interest is served by the effects and example of politicians who would rather be right, whose "nerve of failure" sustains them on their own way, undaunted by the chances of rejection or defeat. Even if he loses more often than others, a politician who peddles the truth is his constituents' gain. And he strengthens their stomach for truth by often repeating the dose.

Part

Leadership among the Leisured

▼

Throughout the country's history the chief boundary between the parties has been changing. Sometimes it has been regional. From 1930 to 1950, the primary fault line separating them was between haves and have-nots. Since then, it has been hard to find. A political fortune awaits the first able politician to locate the next 50-yard line. It may be on the complexities which we have made for ourselves. Perhaps imaginative vs. unimaginative, educated vs. uneducated, boldness vs. caution, conformity vs. nonconformity, closed vs. open mind. Or the difference may depend upon the window through which one sees the world.

The new main division may be between a liberal upper class and a conservative lower one. The economic class system is disappearing. Although it cannot yet be said that redistribution of wealth and income is compressing to a pancake the cone of economic ranks, the combination of the raised floor and the truncation of the tip has ended economic inequality's political significance. At the same time, a new class system on the basis of socially desired talent is being created by the removal of the barriers of race and birth. A person can rise or fall faster and farther than before. The old observation about "shirt sleeves to shirt sleeves" will be contracted from three generations to one, and then will cease to be true because each person can wear the same clothes as anyone else.

The numerical proportion of talented people has not changed, but they used to be scattered through society. Now that persons are allowed to rise or fall to a level which their talents fit, they are developing, through association, a sense of community or class with those whose talents are the same. The growing trend of gifts, either direct or through foundations, from businesses to colleges is an example of the new link between some of the talented people in each, as well as a recognition by business executives that men and women with advanced schooling are needed to manage our economy. The degree of segregated association, creating a sense of class, is increased as family ties are loosened by many causes, including the free choice of companions enabled by technology and social equality, combined with the assignment of people to the station fitted by their capacities. People will tend to have companions more like themselves than are most of their kin. An example is Harlow Curtice and his brother, who were employed by General Motors, one as president and the other as a machinist. They had little to do with each other, although it is said that their mutual feelings were cordial. In the past such brothers probably would have been engaged in similar work, had closely overlapping circles of friends, and often eaten at the same table.

Another cause tending to stratify into a class those on the same level of talent is the awareness of each person that everyone who knows him recognizes that he belongs where he is, while formerly judgment on him was reserved because his ability was not proved by his rank. When impediments have been removed from each person's rise or fall to the level which his ability fits, either he will have no excuse for his low station or he will deserve full credit for his high one. This condition may make people feel more comfortable with others on their own level. Its stratifying force may be stronger upon those on the lower levels, who may feel anxiety and depression at the knowledge that they belong where they are and that this fact is known by all who know them. In the past most persons felt a reservation about scorn for those below because they knew that but for the grace of the social system their positions might be reversed. This coming discomfort between persons on different levels will be mitigated by two things:

First is the recognition that status depends, as always, on background, which determines what as well as who a person is; and recognition that the background factors which determine status have been shifted from social setting to personality, from outer to inner gifts. Second is the greater understanding that now exists between classes. In the past the members of the ruling classes, from Marcus Aurelius to slave traders, hardly saw members of the laboring classes as human beings. And poor folk used to regard some of the nobility as embodiments of more marvelous qualities than they possessed in fact. To some extent the serf would live vicariously through the lord of the manor some aspects of life such as adornment, grace, valor, and the regular eating of meat.

Accurate sifting of abilities will divide society into haves and have-nots of talent rather than wealth. Instead of a sharp division between upper and lower there will be a scale of imperceptible grades from Newton to Jukes. The boundary between the two halves will not run along a gulf.·

The shape of society when classified on the basis of talent will resemble, not an hourglass but a fishing bob, or a pair of coolie hats laid brim to brim, with a spike projecting from the peak of each. In statistical terms it can be described as a pair of normal curves, one on each side of the vertical axis; the mode will be at the mean, and it will be bigger than it used to be in proportion to the whole, and the tapering ends will be correspondingly longer and thinner. More of the people will be clustered near the equator which divides the two classes, or parties. The advent of great wealth equally spread will make people more alike in developed talent than before because there no longer will be some who have enjoyed leisure, education, and experience while others are stunted and kept as hewers of wood. When no one must do long hours of tiring routine work, there will be a more nearly equal chance for each person to exercise and thus develop his mind and skills, even though differences remain in the degree to which people's work requires or permits such exercise while on the job. All people will be equally exposed to the mass media's enlightenment and stimulation.

However, the spread between the two extremes of talent, the spikes at the top and bottom, will be greater than in the past. Those on the south spike, on the level of legal incompetence, are unable to benefit by opportunity and comfort, and so are as low as ever. Those on the north spike will have greater advantages than the most privileged aristocracy of the past: fewer hours of mechanical routine, a higher level of education and, most important of all, the challenge of first-rate company, undiluted by wellborn dolts and drones.

However, these extremes are so small in proportion to the mass in the middle that in politics they do not matter much. The middle will have enough wealth and skills of collective action to take care of the south pole and enough competent leaders, for most things, to be independent of the north. After all, politicians will be a small proportion of those on the upper spike, most of whose occupants are seminal minds which make new worlds, while politics is more concerned with judgment which makes the world go round. Creative thinkers shape more than their share of history, but judgment is what the world pays for and what it looks for when it votes.

With the abolition of inherited titles and all but minimal inherited wealth, the members of the new upper class of talent will not, without a radical reversion to the old ways, be able to pass their status to their children, except by upbringing which assists children to develop their talents and to wish to use them. Nor can these members keep their status for themselves except by their own continued efforts. They will have no vested interest in things as they are except the right to have their talent recognized. Unlike wealth, whether inherited or acquired by effort, talent can neither be given nor taken away by social change. Most of the more bold and imaginative members of society will be among the upper class, which will be more favorable to experiment and less disposed to resist change than the lower class, which will have lost its more daring members to the upper class.

Those who remain in the lower class, or descend to it, will compose a group more stagnant and limited in its thinking than the old working class, which had the leavening of the more able men who used to be a part of it. Manual laborers' residential areas will produce no more folk art. Labor unions now find it difficult to obtain leaders among the younger men. The appeal of class loyalty has gone; so has the goad of class hate. The success and peace of the labor movement have dampened the idealism of all but a few incorrigible zealots. The most gifted of the youth in working class families have left for more rewarding work which has been put within their reach by the removal of hereditary bars. If they have the ability, those who want money go into business or medicine; those who want security join the armed forces, become schoolteachers or get civil service jobs; those who want fame go into entertainment, politics, or sport; those who want idleness, freedom from responsibility, or time for leisure pursuits, work for a big company at short hours; those who want power can get more for the same price in other fields. So the union membership has lost not only most of its potential leaders but also many of the more vigilant members, who do so much to select the best leaders and insure that they perform well. Two likely results are a decline in the number of union leaders and a rise in the average importance of the duties of each.

Soon the working class will vanish upon the full success of its radical demands for civil rights and an equal share of the wealth. Members of the new lower class will not be powerless to try social experiments or press for drastic change, like the most oppressed members of the former working class, who lacked the skills and vigor to apply the necessary force and were resigned by weakness to the fellahin's attitude that hardship and misfortune are Allah's will. They will not be prevented by the upper class from exerting effective pressure to alter the rules and shape of society, except to put themselves above the upper class. Historically, most societies favored some people despite their lack of talent, but it is hard to conceive of a society so irrational that it would raise people because they lacked talent. Furthermore, when it so decided for self-protection, the upper class could exercise preponderant strength against the lower. Although the lower class will not be handicapped by poverty, lack of organization, and extreme ignorance, as was the former laboring class, the upper class will constitute one half of the whole, rather than a small minority, and in revealed ability all the upper class's members will surpass all the lower class, in contrast to the past substantial overlap.

Although unable to make itself dominant, the new lower class will be able to rock the boat, yet it will be composed of persons reluctant to do so. Lacking such a disposition, and without a new incentive to replace the spur of want, the new lower class will lack both hope and need for fundamental change.

The blurred boundaries between horizontal grades will make it easier for each person in the middle ranks to ignore his exact status or to misrepresent it to himself. Social mobility may increase anxiety but reduce discontent. Lower-class resentment against the upper may be stirred by little except a person's knowledge that despite the presence of a marshal's baton in his knapsack he remains a private. If strong frustrations should develop in the lower class and not be relieved by the leadership, it seems probable that there would be a temporary period of violence by the lower class and conservatism by the upper. Except for such aberrations, however, these new conditions will tend to make the upper class liberal and the lower class conservative.

Another cause pushing the lower class toward conservatism in its politics is that it is becoming the more leisured class. Unlike wealth, work is not becoming more evenly shared. The patterns of our technology are changing in a direction which reduces the proportion of unskilled work to skilled work. In relation to skilled persons, fewer unskilled men are necessary to build a rocket ship than a steam ship. The probable result is shorter hours for unskilled jobs in proportion to skilled jobs. By reason of each class's opportunity and choice, the lower class will work less than the upper. As in ages past, idle rich will be supported by others, but by the more able rich instead of by slaves.

With enough abundance, the comparative economic worth of talents becomes less important as a factor in setting work hours than the personal cost of work to the individual. In terms of the person's attitude toward his own time, interesting or pleasant work costs less than dull or disagreeable work. Four hours on a garbage truck are the equivalent of a longer period at a desk in a bank. When everyone has plenty of money a reduction of hours is a more effective improvement in a person's employment conditions than is a raise in pay. Already, some jobs are preferred by some people for the satisfaction or pleasure of their performance despite a lower rate of pay than is available to these people at other jobs. And the elements of competition and joy in work, the incentives for longer hours, are largely confined to skilled work.

With less time at work than the upper class the lower class would spend more time at play. The leisure pursuits of the lower class would be more active, as well as of longer duration, than those of the former laboring class. Always in the past members of the laboring class were uncultivated in the arts of leisure, and when their time came for play they were tired. They lacked both inclination and capacity to do more than reach out one hand to state their preference for another channel or a gladiator's life.

But when members of the lower class can start to play when they wake up in the morning, tired by nothing but yesterday's play, and when they have had a chance to cultivate the arts of leisure, they may engage in more active amusements than were practiced by the former laboring class. Already they have begun. In this respect their choice of amusements may be like that of the dancing, hunting, and conversation practiced by the small leisure classes of the past. With more leisure than the upper class, the members of the lower may give their minds less exercise, while the upper class will have sufficient leisure for its members' minds

to be diverted and relaxed. Insofar as leisure pursuits are fulfilling, and audience participation makes this more likely, and insofar as they do not challenge the critical or imaginative faculties,
greater leisure is likely to cause a more conservative attitude. The
closer horizons of the less-educated tend to raise their resistance
to that change which is not the current whim of the crowd.

Politics will continue to be a vocation of strenuous work. The
dispersion and increase of wealth have expanded the demand for
services from most of the skilled vocations. The capacity to afford professional and administrative services has increased as fast
as the capacity to afford training for those vocations, while the
inclination to prepare for them has declined because the prospect
of the first few years' austerity and effort has offset the appeal of
the extra margin of pay, which is not needed to insure comfort.
Some young people prefer to take the ready cash and forgo the
greater future gain. The present heavy work load in most of these
vocations will be lightened by the spread of the work as the membership in each vocation increases in relation to the total population and to the demand for the vocation's services. However, for
politicians, and for other persons who manage affairs in business,
education, or philanthropy, the days and months of work will be
as long as before. The work load cannot be reduced by spreading
it thinner in those areas where the work cannot be done suffi-
ciently well to meet public needs unless it is given continuous
attention after long and exacting training. In some vocations a
rise in average pay will cut the work load by attracting more persons into the field. But in politics, where much of the work cannot be done well unless concentrated in a comparatively few
hands, an increase in pay may only intensify the competition
and induce politicians to work harder than ever. Of course, it may
be in the public interest to attract more persons into politics so
as to raise the quality of the best among them. But if politics
becomes a squirrel cage in comparison to other vocations the in-
ducements to enter politics may not attract the best people, and
in the future a pay raise is not likely to be a powerful bait.

Furthermore, in politics the competition makes each participant drive the rest to harder, more continuous work. It is difficult to conceive of making politics less competitive without either making it stagnant or shifting some of its functions to another field, where the problem would be renewed.

In some vocations an imposed limitation of hours would protect practitioners from being beaten out for the prizes by the more industrious and therefore would encourage compliance with the rules. But in politics limitations on hours, whether agreed, decreed, or legislated, would be unenforceable if tried and against the public interest if successful.

The device of sabbatical years, however, might alleviate the comparatively harsh terms of labor in politics. While it is not practical to blow a whistle, making politicians quit work three hours after lunch, each politician for a full year during the middle of his term could be prohibited, on penalty of forfeiting his office, from appearing at any scene where public policy is formed or set in motion. Such absences would not appreciably impair their capacity to perform in office and in some ways would improve it. Instead of merely throwing the rascals out, we may in the future throw out the good ones too, at regular intervals, inviting them to have a rest and then come back.

▼

The accuracy of the new class pattern's personnel placement will tend to identify as such those persons who combine intelligence and honesty in the highest degree. These persons may contribute substantially to forming general public opinion about subjects in their own respective fields. Their leadership in opinion formation will be greater than it has been in recent years, when most people have had enough knowledge with which to form a basis for an opinion and yet have been uncertain who were the real and reliable experts. These accurately labeled masters in their field may come to lead opinion to a greater extent than has been done by any one since the days when ignorance forced most people to

form their opinions on subjects beyond their experience in re-
liance on some leading members of the ruling class.

Intellectuals may be expected to shift their political alliance
from the underprivileged poor, who will disappear as a class, to
the able, most of whom will have above-average incomes, or whatever will have become the measure of success.

Substantially more than half of the Jews may be expected to
be found in the upper class. It is ironic that not until now can
the Jews be thought a superior people, whether chosen by God
or by chance. In antiquity their contribution to civilization,
though substantial, was not comparable to what the Greeks and
Romans did; between then and the recent past they lived in isolation and obscurity with modest accomplishments for a time in
Spain, later in Turkey, Holland, and elsewhere. They were out-
shone by the Normans and by other gentile groups in Italy and
France. But the exclusion of non-Christians from land ownership
forced Jews to live in the towns and thereby become adapted to
urban culture. This head start gave a cumulative advantage to
their descendants. Perhaps an even stronger factor is that urban
life under persecution made them the only recognizable group in
the world which has been subject to the process of natural selection on the basis of brains for a period of enough generations for
it to take effect. At the same time, they retained their straight and
narrow outlook longer, emerging late from their form of Middle
Ages, and now are in a delayed renaissance. Thus, in most of
those areas of endeavor which we think important there is, and
for a while in America there will continue to be, soaring achievement, not of Judaism but by Jews.

▼

This new class system already has collided with the American
tradition of a politician's identification with the community
which elects him. The top grades of talent have become concentrated in urban centers of thought, renown, and wealth, while
Congressmen still are elected according to population on an even

geographic spread. Before the turn of the century, in "The American Commonwealth," Bryce observed this condition which ever since has grown less necessary and more acute.

The dissolution of roots in the community of one's birth has refined and accelerated the sifting process. While the centripetal force of urban centers has drawn able men on a small scale for centuries, only since they could support themselves there have talented women been free to go; now to the gifted of both sexes the big cities are like the sea to the lemmings or the Gadarene swine. Because the talented have migrated to the metropolitan centers in a higher proportion than the untalented, the merit of the average office holder in relation to the importance of the office is lower in the U. S. House of Representatives than in any other public employment, possibly excepting some police forces.

By custom, though not by law, a well-established residence in the district still is a condition of election to the House, even though the conflicts of regional interest have relaxed, and each cluster of communities no longer preserves in isolation a distinctive nature calling for loyalty and understanding which can come only from a deep attachment. The rise in the rate at which persons shift their homes is contracting the time period required to establish enough local identity to qualify for Congress. However, the wait still is substantial in all districts and longest in those long-settled, half-deserted areas where the supply of talent is most short.

Every state has urban centers which, in a lesser degree, stand to the rest of the state as Paris has stood to the rest of France. The Senate does not have to take a crop from many barren zones. But many Congressional districts have no large town and no college that deserves the name. Young men and women worth their salt depart when done with school, returning only for visits of sentimental condescension. Those left behind are persons tending to lack education and imagination, indifferent to the world and how it works. One of them, perhaps the best, goes to Congress to shake the earth. In most of these districts voters receive little choice. The country stands to gain if more young persons equipped for national problems take the gamble of settling in the provinces. If they do not, either the residential requirement will be removed, as in England, or the authority of the House will drop.

In state legislatures, for other reasons, the situation sometimes is reversed. Leading men and women in rural areas go to the legislature, while many of the most able people drawn to the big cities disdain such offices. Country folk may be behind the city in comprehension of public affairs but they are more discriminating in their choice of candidates for the legislature because they know them as neighbors. In metropolitan areas candidates for the legislature tend to be overlooked at the foot of the ballot. Despite these variant factors, the legislatures, like the House, themselves are harmed by the geographic disparity in apportionment between offices and talent.

▼

Unlike the way it has been when both classes produced leaders, under the new system political leaders will come only from the upper class. Leaders may be born of parents in the lower class, or of one parent in each, but before they become leaders they become identified with the upper class. Formerly, men of working class parents could attain this identification, if ever, only after the achievement of leadership.

The leaders of the lower class are not likely to be treated as traitors to their own upper class because class differences will not be as bitter. One reason is that the free flow up and down and the narrow range of variations in revealed ability among members of the great majority will make class difference less sharp. Also, the classes will be equally free and well fed, and the people on different levels of talent will be closer in many ways than were the social classes of the past. All people will have greater understanding, and therefore sympathy, for persons on other levels of talent than used to be the case between classes whose members lived like different species. Certain common interests draw people together along slanting lines which intersect the planes of talent. These same interests tend to divide people who are on the same talent level and thus to reduce the solidarity of class antagonism.

These leaders of the new lower class will try to climb even higher in the upper class by promoting the interests of the lower. They will choose to become leaders of the lower class for two motives: preference for the conservative philosophy, and the wish for a position of leadership in a field where the number of such positions in both classes is limited and of about equal desirability in each. The latter motive always has been present. As a primary motive the former will have succeeded the old sense of injustice to be righted; in the past a personal preference for the liberal philosophy has been a factor which induced a patrician to advocate the cause of the working class.

When everyone lives on the same levels of comfort and opportunity there will be no more leaders from deprived beginnings and no more voters awed by the comparative majesty of their leaders' station. Among leaders of the same rank there no longer will be a wide range in the length and steepness of the ladders which they have climbed. For voters living in comfort, aware that the leaders are not much better off than they, there is less need to live through some splendid figure of a leader. So perhaps people will choose leaders who are more like than superior to themselves, who are of the upper class but not far up. After the 1920 election Wilson Mizner remarked that he had not realized until then the truth of his mother's reminder to him as a child that anyone can be elected President. Now maybe both aspects of this double meaning will become the common custom.

The policy issues between the parties formed by these two classes will not be comparative comforts or rights to take part in government; they will be the manner of approach to all problems, perhaps an opposition of liberal vs. conservative (as distinguished from the present secondary division of sentimental humanitarianism vs. decayed liberalism and a vision of the old days looking splendid in the dusk with the light behind them). It may be that more than half of the liberal leaders will be found in policy-making positions in the executive branch, which has become the main originating source, while a greater proportion of conservative leaders may go into the legislative branch, which in its now reversed position primarily vetoes, approves, adjusts, and corrects.

Whatever the basis of division between the parties in the future, it is certain only that the line will not be between dumb and smart, or bad and good, with all wisdom or virtue on one side. This approach has been the ground for separation in the eyes of narrow partisans. As upon the extinction of the Federalist and Whig Parties, followed promptly by a Democratic Party split, a patent concentration of merit does not last because it attracts the whole electorate, and so the process of division into two disputing parts has to start again.